What
they're saying
about

Community
Conversations

"I work from the firm belief that 'whatever the problem, community is the answer.' *Community Conversations* teaches us how to make that statement true. The stories, examples, and processes gathered together in one lovely book hopefully will inspire you to become active in creating the conversations that will weave our communities into health and new capacity."

> — **MARGARET J. WHEATLEY**, author of *Leadership and the New Science*; *Turning to One Another: Simple Conversations to Restore Hope to the Future*; and other books

"Born's book is a summary of many experiences and experiments in community conversations. His distillation of what has worked for him, tricks and formats to use, and principles to follow will be valuable for anyone who works in this fascinating, challenging, diverse, and emergent space."

> — **TREVOR GRAY**, Executive Director,
> The Tindall Foundation, New Zealand

"Paul Born's *Community Conversations* draws from decades of experience to illuminate the strong and effective ideas that emerge when diverse participants meet together over well-mediated conversations. The book is replete with inspirational stories and how-to tips, delivered with clear writing, gentle humor, and reflective commentary that provides powerful insights into community-based dialogue."

— **MARK L. WINSTON**, Academic Director and Fellow, Center for Dialogue, Simon Fraser University

"Paul Born has done a masterful job of demonstrating the power of community conversations. The combination of first-hand stories, concepts that make sense, and practical advice will make this a favorite book for community leaders, facilitators, and activists."

— **BRENDA ZIMMERMAN**, co-author of *Getting to Maybe: How the World Is Changed*, and Director of the Health Industry Management Program and Associate Professor of Strategy/Policy at Schulich School of Business

"I appreciate Born's efforts to break collaboration down into its constituent parts and to elevate its skills and knowledge to an art form deserving of our close attention. We need to walk the talk more often in more meetings and more projects in order to instill the skills of listening, creativity, non-judgment, visioning, and collaborative leadership (and 'followership') at every level of community life."

— **MICHELLE COLUSSI**, Canadian Center for Community Renewal, author of "Seven Prerequisites of Transformation" in *Making Waves* (vol. 20, no. 1)

"Written by someone who has walked the talk, this book makes a compelling case that working collaboratively in traditionally unorthodox alliances can achieve great things in the most deprived communities. A highly recommended handbook for all communities."
— HELEN WILSON, *Inspiring Communities Network News*, New Zealand, July 2008

"This slim volume explores a new kind of social dialogue emerging in communities across North America. Born is a social entrepreneur and co-founder of Vibrant Communities, whose work is at the forefront of social change movements in Canada. An engaging storyteller and speaker, Born is inspirational and humble. Here he offers us stories and practices — including Future Search and Conversation Cafés — that can bring communities together into conversations and collaborations that will shift the ways we approach our intractable and increasingly complex social issues."
— Editor's Choice, *ascent magazine* (winter 2008)

"*Community Conversations* dispels the notion that talk is cheap. Talking and good conversations are essential to rethinking our analysis, our partners, and our actions as we tackle our tough social and ecological challenges. You can imagine yourself as an impresario of good conversation after reading this book."
— AL ETMANSKI, Founder of Planned Lifetime Advocacy Network and author of *A Good Life*

"Born's success in facilitating community conversations that really make a difference to community well-being and people's lives comes shining through. His visionary and strategic approach, combined with real-life experience, handy hints, and practical tools, makes for fascinating reading. This is a book to go back to time and time again."
— **MARY-JANE RIVERS**, Inspiring Communities, New Zealand

"My students responded so well to your book and you. *Community Conversations* is a valuable contribution and deserves to be well promoted. Many of the students have gone on to explore the Tamarack contributions, so it is a win-win."
— **DAVID NOSTBAKKEN**, Professor, School of Journalism and Mass Communication, Carleton University

"Paul Born is a change maker. If you want to understand how to make change happen, explore the techniques he uses to enable communities to take charge of their own future."
— **JUDITH MAXWELL**, Founder and Senior Fellow, Canadian Policy Research Networks (CPRN)

"I love *Community Conversations* because I think it will be helpful to our ever-emerging Canadian Community for Dialogue and Deliberation, among other communities. It is an easy read, packed with such simple yet strong lessons which we all have acquired in our practices yet tend to forget or let slide to the sides of our frames of action, let alone reference."
— **SANDRA ZAGON**, Past-Chair, Canadian Community for Dialogue and Deliberation

"I found in *Community Conversations* a profound 'identité de vue' (same passion) with the author's perspective — in particular, 'we listened and gained a corner on the obvious,' which translated is 'nous écoutons et tentons de capter ce qui est evident.' This describes our work in the community very well."

— **LYSE BRUNET**, Directrice générale,
Québec Enfants, Fondation Lucie et André Chagnon

"*Community Conversations* is appropriately conversational in its style, making it enjoyable and easy to read. Usually, we think of conversations occurring in very typical or traditional ways. Born reminds us that there are a multitude of ways in which communities can converse and that by being creative in our approach to these interactions, a greater opportunity exists for our communities to be inspired and involved."

— **SALIMA STANLEY-BHANJI**, Director,
Vibrant Communities Calgary

"If you work within communities, this book can give you more knowledge, encouragement, and hope in order to do so better. There are new ideas and clear outlines of the steps you can take to try new approaches in community engagement. I found it to be truly inspiring and will return to it over and over again when I need to reflect and find new ways of connecting to people."

— **JANICE MELNYCHUK**, Executive Director,
Vibrant Communities Edmonton

"Through simplification of complex concepts and illustrative and relevant examples, Born has succeeded in whetting the reader's appetite to do more for his/her community. Many of the tips outlined in the book are easily reproduced and can help to guarantee the successful development of multi-stakeholder working groups. The well-defined chapters allow the reader to come back to specific areas of discussion to highlight solutions to challenges they may experience along the way."

— **SUSAN SCOTTI**, Senior Assistant Deputy Minister, Human Resources and Skills Development Canada (HRSDC)

"I spent the day yesterday with your book and I am energized! You have spoken exactly of some of the things that have been rattling around in my mind over the past year about the disconnect between people and groups based on a need for a new awareness of what it means to listen and to dialogue. Your book has given me ideas on how I can improve some of our practitioner-training workshops and annual conversation cafes. I honestly feel that literacy practitioners who read the book have the potential to change the landscape of our province. Very exciting."

— **CONNIE JONES**, Adult Literacy Coordinator, Saskatchewan Literacy Network

"Facilitated conversations among people from diverse walks of life are a building block for social advancement. In *Community Conversations* Born offers informative and inspiring examples of multi-stakeholder collaboration that have led to reducing poverty and crime and to re-energizing citizens and social programs."

— *What's Budding @ Maytree*, August 2008

"If you want to help your community move from good to better, this book is a must read. Born draws the reader into some marvelous conversations about the theory and techniques that lie behind community improvements."

— **MONICA CHAPERLIN**, Coordinator,
Business Community Anti-Poverty Initiative

**Learn more about Paul Born and *Community Conversations*
at: http://www.paulborn.ca**

Community Conversations

Mobilizing the Ideas, Skills, and Passion
of Community Organizations, Governments,
Businesses, and People

SECOND EDITION

PAUL BORN

Toronto and New York

Second edition published in 2012 by
BPS Books
Toronto & New York
www.bpsbooks.net
A division of Bastian Publishing Services Ltd.

In association with
Tamarack — An Institute
for Community Engagement
www.tamarackcommunity.ca

ISBN 978-1-927483-15-2

First edition published by BPS Books in 2008

Typesetting: Greg Devitt Design

To my family — Marlene, Lucas, Michael —
and our extended community:
How I enjoy our conversations

Special thanks to Dr. Joseph Schaeffer,
dialogue guru, mentor, and friend

Contents

Part II / Ten Techniques for Community Conversations

Introduction to Part II

Preface

I am delighted to see this book published in this second edition — revised and updated to reflect its growing international readership. Over 12,000 copies of the first edition have been sold. What a joy it has been for me to see the book in the hands of so many people who are conversing with individuals and groups in their community to solve problems, meet challenges, and grow together in new and surprising ways.

More than a decade ago, Alan Broadbent of the Avana Capital Corporation and the Maytree Foundation sat with me at his "partners desk" (designed for two people working across from each other), and we talked. The conversation lasted nearly six months — well, not all of it at that desk — and together we agreed to form Tamarack - An Institute for Community Engagement. The key purpose of Tamarack is to discover new ways for communities to work together and find solutions to some of the pressing problems they are facing. Hence this book, because conversations of diverse kinds, at the community level, are the very engine room of fulfilling that purpose. *Community Conversations* fits the ethos, mandate, and dreams of Tamarack and everyone and everything it touches.

Early in our work we joined with Tim Brodhead (President) and Katharine Pearson of the J.W. McConnell Family Foundation and Sherri Torjman of the Caledon Institute of Social Policy to form Vibrant Communities, a national network of communities seeking innovative and collaborative ways to end poverty. Many of our partner cities spent more than a year in conversation with their communities to form multi-sector networks and to agree on what needed to change if they were to truly reduce poverty. Collectively, these conversations have now reduced poverty in the lives of more than 202,000 families (for more on this, go to www.vibrantcommunites.ca).

This was a fun book to write. It came easily to me because I love conversations — especially big, messy, and purposeful ones. Joining me on this journey — people to whom I am forever indebted — were Rachel Veira Gainer, who brought amazing editing skills, positive energy, and great enthusiasm to the project; Louise Kearney and Mark Cabaj, whom I worked with for more than a decade and whose ideas permeate what you're about to read; Liz Weaver, who is leading our poverty-reduction work; Laura Zikovic, for her graphics skills; Donald G. Bastian of BPS Books, who has done an amazing job of turning the manuscript into a real book; a myriad of readers and Tamarack supporters, too many to mention; and the entire Tamarack team, for their ideas and support.

Simply put, the book you have in your hands is the result of what we've learned from observing and facilitating conversations. My assumption is that you are already working hard to make your communities great places to live. I want to thank you for your tireless efforts and optimism. I feel connected to your work and hope that it will be enhanced as you join in the journey of this book. I also hope that we will connect someday. In the meantime, please visit www.tamarackcommunity.ca to stay in touch.

Introduction:
A New Era in
Community Building

A new kind of social dialogue is emerging in communities around the world. These conversations — I call them community conversations — are being generated by two conflicting realities: the growing complexity of our societies' needs and the elementary nature of the tools available to fix them.

The issues facing communities and those at risk — the unemployed, disabled persons, single parents, and senior citizens, to name a few — are complex. Yet the system that serves those in need yields simplistic solutions. Services such as counseling, income support, and housing are calibrated to solve single issues. They are sorely lacking in the face of personal and community problems that are multifaceted, adaptive, and interconnected.

Individuals who suddenly find themselves without a job, for example, face a bewildering array of single-issue services to call on.

One organization provides job-search counseling, another job training, while the income-support agency and social security office are at opposite ends of town. All too often even basic necessities, such as food and clothing, are provided by separate agencies. The people at risk, however, often face a multitude of personal and social issues, such as their community's economic status and safety, and its attitudes toward racism. Is it any wonder that they are frustrated with a community system that, for example, offers band-aid solutions like food vouchers, instead of diagnosing and treating the root causes of social ills, such as a lack of sustainable employment?

But things are changing. Our inability to address these challenges head-on has led some communities to enter into unprecedented conversations about how the community system needs to change. These conversations are beginning to focus on finding a better way forward. Funding cuts or changing government priorities may have prompted this search, but change has also been sparked by community leaders who are seeking more comprehensive, effective solutions.

I have written *Community Conversations* for those who are responsible to form and lead these conversations and those who have committed themselves to participate in them. I hope to help make community conversations as easy, enjoyable, and effective as possible.

Appropriately enough, I have chosen to write this book conversationally. As you will see, I love telling stories. In fact, recalling some of the best conversations I have been involved in has sustained me on this writing journey.

What to Expect from This Book

Community Conversations is composed of two parts. Part I is theoretical, but gently so. Using anecdotes and concrete examples, it explores the four building blocks of community conversations: conversing, engaging, collaborating, and casting a vision. Part II gets down to specifics, with ten stories of great community conversations that I have been part of. These stories will give you proven techniques for holding deliberate and strategic conversations where you live.

Most of the chapters are relatively short. They may be read in sequence or as your interest leads you. My hope is that the stories I share will inspire you and help you see the many ways to be creative in solving social issues.

Resources worth exploring for further information are included at the end of the book. To make these more convenient for you to access, we have placed this section on the Tamarack website at www.tamarack community.ca. Or you can e-mail us at tamarack@tamarackcommunity.ca for an electronic version. We will continually update the content to reflect new or revised links, resources, and learnings.

~

One piece of context-setting is needed before we begin our journey together. It has to do with the recent social movement called Comprehensive Community Initiatives (CCIs), a movement that is leading the drive toward better, more comprehensive solutions to the complex issues of our communities today. CCIs work across sectoral boundaries because the people involved recognize that issues such as racism and poverty can be addressed only if problems and solutions are aligned. CCIs, according to the Aspen Institute's Roundtable on Community Change (1997),

> *seek improved outcomes for individuals and families,*
> *as well as improvements in neighborhood conditions,*
> *by working comprehensively across social, economic*
> *and physical sectors. CCIs operate on the principle*
> *that community building — that is, strengthen-*
> *ing institutional capacity at the community level,*
> *enhancing social capital and personal networks, and*
> *developing leadership — is a necessary aspect of the*
> *process of transforming issues facing a community.*

When a community begins to think and work comprehensively, it naturally attempts to use all of its assets. Assets can take different forms and come from surprising places. Schools, businesses, government departments, museums, community centers, and parks and other public spaces can provide resources, ideas, and support. But most often it is not the organizations but the people who lead them that represent the true, untapped asset. For instance, the clients served by an initiative bring unique and passionate ideas; the director and volunteers of organizations bring valuable perspectives and a web of relationships; and the business community or people at different levels of government bring new ideas, talents, and financial resources.

What I am attempting to contribute, through this book, is the insight that effective community conversations are the *means* by which CCIs are more likely to be successful. Through this type of conversation, we bring together the ideas, skills, passions, and hopes of all sectors of the community. And we forge a better path forward, creating a network of people committed to advancing the idea.

These conversations usually begin with a small group of people. As this group deepens their understanding of and commitment to their goals, they reach out to engage their broader community, building a larger, multi-sector network. This network spends significant time in conversation, learning about the issues they hope to solve and building trust and a common language across sectors. Most often, but not always, a vision emerges that all of these sectors resonate with, a formal leadership roundtable is formed, and a community plan is written.

At this stage, a community conversation takes on two purposes. The first is to create a space in which those involved can to get to know, understand, and trust one another. Trust is important because it allows people to open up to new ideas and suspend what they know to be true. The second purpose is to create a space to learn together. In some ways, the space we create together is like a ship for exploring new seas. A key outcome of conversation is the ability of a diverse group of people to come to a common understanding.

The role of these conversations is to bring together the people in a community who can contribute to the success of the initiative being promoted. By working together, people can change the way a community addresses a particular issue, improving the quality of life on many levels. Like a tide that lifts all boats, community conversations enable real and lasting community change.

Part I

THE BUILDING BLOCKS OF
COMMUNITY CONVERSATIONS

Introduction to Part I

It was a cold winter day where I live. There was talk of a snow-storm that would close the city down. In spite of this warning, forty people sat in a large, windowless room in a library basement talking about the harsh reality of poverty. Outside the room, eager to capture the story that was unfolding, a reporter and camera crew were waiting for the group to break.

The conversation started slowly but, like the storm outside, soon enough began to escalate. The event was so engaging that the Regional Chair (the Mayor) returned to the meeting after two hours away to deal with a storm-induced state of emergency. Even though the City was battening down in the face of the storm, he and thirty-nine others did not want to miss the opportunity before them.

For more than two days, these people — ten each from business, government, community agencies, and people living in poverty — embarked on a journey of dialogue.

I had held hundreds — no, thousands — of meetings in my life. I was a trained facilitator and an experienced meeting chair. When planning this gathering, I thought, "Let's just bring them together and let them talk." We engaged Doug Bowie, a former oil executive who is known for his great skill in a dialogue technique called Future Search, to help us.

In the months before this intense conversation began, Doug and I had our own ongoing conversation. "Why do you want to bring these people together?" he asked me. "What will they talk about? Who will you bring together? Will the group be able to answer the questions you're asking? What will they talk about that will keep their attention for two days?"

After I rattled off my standard answers to his many questions, he continued with a few more: "What do you think will change after holding this conversation? What do you think will compel people to change?"

"Good questions," I thought, remaining silent.

Doug taught me a lot as we prepared for this conversation. He taught me to be deliberate about the intended purpose of the conversation. We spent days just getting the question right, and several weeks planning the invitation list. Doug repeatedly asked, "Are these the people who, once they agree on a path forward, will have the ability to influence the system to change the way we need it to change?" We agonized over every detail.

When we shared what we had planned with the community, our idea received immediate attention from the media. They realized that this was more than just a bunch of people talking: It was a unique mix of people embarking on a structured journey. They understood that, if this group agreed on a path forward, things would change.

As the storm raged outside over the next two days, we deconstructed the history of poverty in the community, analyzed the current reality, and then created a new vision and path forward for what was possible. Doug was attentive to the energy in the room, the success of every exercise, and all the details — even of every break.

"He's an oil company executive?" I thought. "He should be a wedding planner!"

The media continued to be fascinated by the event. The local paper published stories daily, and the local television station gave the event plenty of screen time, airing live at every break and running feature stories on the six o'clock news. Recognizing the community's interest in the topic and the group's approach, print and electronic media alike featured the ramifications of the dialogue for a whole month, including through a three-part documentary on poverty and ten feature stories in the local paper.

This was no ordinary conversation. As Doug is fond of saying, "There are conversations and there are *conversations*."

1

CONVERSING

Call miracle, self-healing:
The utter, self-revealing
Double-take of feeling.
If there's fire on the mountain
Or lightning and storm
And a god speaks from the sky

That means someone is hearing
The outcry and the birth—cry
Of new life at its term.

~ Seamus Heaney,
"Doubletake," The Cure at Troy

The following experience forever changed my understanding of what a community conversation could and should be.

Several years ago, the government of Northern Ireland invited my colleagues and me to visit their community. At the time, I was director of the Community Opportunities Development Association (CODA) in Waterloo Region, Ontario. For many years we had brought, to our area, young people involved in or influenced by the Troubles in Ireland to improve their job skills, build relationships, and see how Catholics and Protestants lived together peacefully. Now it was our turn to visit the people and projects that our organization had affected.

Many of the young people we had worked with had either joined or were thinking of joining the Irish Republic Army or the Ulster Freedom Fighters. We knew this by the tattoos on their arms.

We arrived in Northern Ireland at the height of the Troubles. Bombings and retaliations for murders were happening weekly. I was energized by the prospect of reconnecting with the many young people who had visited us, but was also worried for our safety. We were surprised when our taxi driver casually said, when dropping us off at our hotel, "Oh, you're staying here? This place is newly renovated because it was bombed recently." It was a nice hotel, but needless to say, I did not sleep well that night.

The following night, I watched a report of a recent homicide, on a local TV news program. A taxi driver had been shot at three a.m. while drinking coffee in his predominantly Catholic neighborhood: a neighborhood we were scheduled to visit. The attack was one of retaliation.

The next morning, we set off on a tour, led by a government official, to see a community organization in the Brookfield area of northern Belfast. We were also going to meet the organization's director, Father Cavanaugh.

As we neared the site, we were taken aback by the high walls on either side of the road.

"They call this the Gaza strip," the government official told us. "Catholics live on one side and Protestants on the other. The walls protect them from people climbing up on their roofs and shooting at their neighbors." He said he had never stopped on this road before.

As we entered the gate that led us into the community center complex — with barbed wire hovering above us on top of the walls — we were greeted by an armed guard. He escorted us to Father Cavanaugh, who was busy, perhaps distracted, and, as I recall, a bit rude. He said we would have lunch later and quickly arranged for a member of the community to take us on a tour. We were a bit put off by his curtness, but what we saw over the next several hours changed our mood considerably.

The building we were in had been converted from an old flax mill. The entire mill, composed of three four-story buildings, was now a community center with schools, an international trade center, shops, restaurants, and even a community theater. The place was full of life, and the sheer volume of activities created a profound sense of hope.

We left the compound and entered a mall built by the community center to attract business to the area and keep local wealth in the community. Our guide told us that the grocery store anchored the mall. The storeowners had agreed to locate there after a handshake labor agreement was struck with the IRA and UFF. The two militant groups agreed that if an equal number of Protestants and Catholics were hired and could work separate shifts, they would refrain from blowing up the store for five years.

On our way back to the mill for lunch, we walked past more stores and a significant health center, also developed by the community center. By this time we were hungry not only for lunch but also for the wisdom and story of the man we were about to meet — the man who had envisioned this remarkable place; the man who had seemingly defied all obstacles to build this admirable organization within this needy community.

A variety of people from the community gathered at the table for lunch. We ate, shared stories, and talked about the community and its history. Father Cavanaugh did most of the talking. He had a way with words, and when he became passionate about his work it was hard to get a word in. Father Cavanaugh knew this was an opportunity to sell his organization to the government official, who had access to significant funding.

As we finished lunch and relaxed over coffee, I watched for a moment in the almost sixty minutes of non-stop stories from Father Cavanaugh when I could ask a question.

As he was about to start another story, I blurted out, "Father Cavanaugh, this place is remarkable!"

Realizing that he was about to receive a compliment, he allowed me to continue.

"Father Cavanaugh, we are so impressed by your work and all that you have accomplished, under conditions that are unthinkable to us," I said. Finally I had his attention. "How did you do it? How did all of this come together in these very difficult conditions?"

Father Cavanaugh smiled. He looked around the room at his colleagues and said with a knowing smile, "We listened and gained a corner on the obvious."

His response took me by surprise. I was perplexed but dared not share what was on my mind.

Listen? I thought. Father Cavanaugh has probably never taken an effective listening course in his life. He must mean something else — perhaps a technique *called* listening.

Hurrying to keep his attention, I asked, "What does that mean: listening to gain a corner on the obvious?" But I had lost my chance. He changed the topic, and after he told several more stories, we were dismissed to visit another site.

All this happened more than a decade ago, and I am still exploring the meaning of his simple statement about listening to gain a corner on the obvious.

Conversation

Gaining a corner on the "obvious": Easy to see or understand because not concealed, difficult or ambiguous. Also known as clear, understandable, palpable, noticeable, apparent, evident, observable.
— Encarta Dictionary

Dialogue and listening. One should always follow the other and, in turn, create a good conversation. This is what I had been taught. But what if the objective of listening was more than having a good conversation? What if there was a conversation that went beyond talking? What if the objective of listening and dialogue was to change our communities for the better? What if there were many opposing views about what a better community might be? How would we listen?

For Father Cavanaugh, listening in the form of a conversation was not always possible. Remember, the Brookfield neighborhood had emerged from many years of hatred and mistrust. Listening, without a doubt, meant being heard. Words held many meanings. For the people of Brookfield, trust would be established only through conversations that led to action. The process of listening and being heard had a purpose: to bring about ideas for the kind of change that was best for all.

This experience helped me — as I hope it will help you — to rethink the purpose of a good conversation and to look beyond what a conversation is usually thought to be.

Conversation is not just what is said; it is also what happens between people. Conversation is not always about an event or a time; it is part of a much larger process of change. It leads to more conversation and is a part of a journey to understand. Community conversations are a deliberate form of listening to the people in a community in an effort to learn to agree, to become committed and engaged, and to create a place in which discovering the obvious is possible.

Listening!
Very good, Paul! Now, when you share back what you heard, put a bit more empathy into it ...
— An affirmation (of sorts) from my counseling teacher

I took a course on effective listening as part of my college training to become an organizational leader. I was taught that this type of listening was the ability to repeat what I had just heard in my own words. My professor called it "active listening."

The course was helpful but left me wanting more. Active listening felt artificial to me: a technique to express empathy that somehow did not feel genuine.

We may talk and listen every day, but these simple actions are often the most important — and most difficult — tasks to do when building community.

I believe Father Cavanaugh understood that listening requires much more than just hearing what is said. If asked, he no doubt could have told many stories to illustrate this wisdom. He might have talked about the act of listening. But this certainly wouldn't have been the whole story. I think his story would be about how to engage with the ideas we hear and the people who share them.

Listening, therefore, could be better stated as *Listening!* The exclamation mark denotes listening that leads to dialogue and active engagement. This emphasis gives the word a different meaning from what I was taught in college.

Listening! is much more in tune with the kind of listening that gains a corner on the obvious in order to build a community. In the midst of competing interests and experts who think they know what should be done, and in the pain and joy of working in community, I would love to be the one who actually knew what to do — the one who could actually see the obvious path forward. If only such a magic formula existed!

Several years ago, I was asked to "take a look" at Surrey, British Columbia. While visiting there, I asked a group of social agencies to take me on a tour of the community. In one morning they showed me the needle exchange clinic, low-income housing units, prostitutes' corners, and just about every other place that screamed that Surrey was suffering. Their message was clear.

But the afternoon told a different story. A group of civic leaders and business people led me through some unique cultural establishments, the booming business core, beautiful parks, and influential educational institutions. These sites sent a message, too, giving a glimpse of a community filled with energy and promise.

That evening, I gathered with the two groups to talk more about Surrey. Everyone agreed that the city had problems, but they also agreed that it was a good place to live — that they appreciated being part of the community. We put the community's challenges into perspective by weighing its weaknesses against its strengths. Most importantly, we listened and spoke to one another.

We determined in that meeting that much could be done if we worked together. Though we did not agree on what that was, we had heard enough to know that everyone had an opinion. This was a good starting point, mainly because it opened us to one another's stories and allowed us to see that there were no simple answers. The situation was messy and complex, but we were open to *Listening!* and decided to meet regularly.

The goal of our meetings was not just to talk and listen, or attempt to agree on what we wanted to do, although that is most often what we did. Our goal was to create a space in which we could continue the conversation and take action.

Our dialogue took on two purposes, as described in the introduction to this book. The first was to create this space in order to know, understand, and trust one another. The second was to learn together. Trust allowed us open up to new ideas and suspend what, from our individual perspectives, we held to be true. We hoped that this kind of journey might lead us toward gaining a corner on the obvious.

A key element of gaining a corner on the obvious is the ability of a diverse group of people to come to a common understanding over time. This group may include individuals who have previously mistrusted one another or with whom they have nothing in common.

In Surrey, the voluntary sector and the business community each believed that their understanding of the community was the right one. When people from these two sectors embarked on a journey to understand one another and to build trust, they were able to explore what they had in common and discover new ideas. When the two sectors talked to each other, came to understand the root causes of the issues, and then committed to action, they were much closer to the obvious. They were *Listening!*

A system of seeking agreement can play an important role in helping a community gain a corner on the obvious.

In Surrey, the system was made up of those affected by poverty and those who were affecting it (both positively and negatively). Broadly speaking, this system was made up of employers, government officials, voluntary sector organizations, and people living in poverty.

In Belfast, the system was composed of the IRA, UFF, neighbors, and organizations established to serve the community.

Whether in Surrey, Belfast, or anywhere else, when people who make up the system affecting the issue agree on what to do to improve that system, the chance of actually achieving change is greatly increased.

My experience in Belfast had a profound effect on me. It required me to rethink — or, more importantly, to *unthink* — the way I worked to build my own community. It inspired me to embark on a journey to understand the meaning of community conversations.

What Are Community Conversations?

So, if you are thinking of meeting in a group, one thing I would suggest is to have a discussion or seminar about dialogue for a while, and those who are interested can then go on and have a dialogue. And, you mustn't worry too much whether you are or are not having dialogue, that is one of the blocks. It may be mixed.
— David Bohm, *On Dialogue*

In my work we spend a lot of time in groups, talking and planning in hopes of working better together. We take workshops on effective team performance; we set rules of engagement and exercise conflict management; and we even assess meetings after they are completed. But we rarely talk about what we do ninety-five percent of the time we are together, which is engage in dialogue or conversation. The concepts I share below have been particularly helpful to me, grounding me in my role as a community conversation facilitator. Sometimes, before participating in a dialogue, I return to the thinking that has gone into this section of the book — primarily as a reminder to suspend my judgment.

About Dialogue

Dialogue comes from the Greek words "dia" and "logos," the first meaning "through" and the second "word" or "meaning." The combination of these words is generally accepted to mean "the flow of meaning between people" — or in modern parlance, "information flow."

I find this simple interpretation very helpful. When we are talking with others, *there is a flow of meaning between us*: the place where our ideas and the meaning system we bring to them and others' ideas and the meaning system they bring to them meet. This helps me consider not just the words and statements that are exchanged, but the meaning of the words from the perspective of the persons sharing them. Our meaning systems come from our experience and learning and shape our thinking and beliefs.

The well-known physicist David Bohm has delved deeply into the nature of dialogue and is often cited by those writing on the topic today. He shares one of the most useful descriptions of the value of effective dialogue when he says, "Dialogue is the collective way of opening up judgments and assumptions" (David Bohm, *On Dialogue*). When we open up our judgments and assumptions, we are able to move to another stage in the conversation. Instead of "convincing" others or proving that we are right, we have the opportunity to speak with others and build on their ideas as we engage in *their* meaning.

Why is it so hard to engage in someone else's meaning? Because our own meaning comes into play, and with meaning comes assumptions. I assume that because you are white, you do not know what it is like to experience racism. I assume that because you are rich, you do not know what it is like to be poor. I assume that because you are in business, you care for nothing but the bottom line. I assume that because you have power, you do not know what it is like to be powerless.

We speak and listen through our assumptions. These assumptions are not easy to overcome. They are the ropes that bind together our belief systems.

Suspend Your Assumptions, and Engage in Meaning

In a training exercise, Joe Schaeffer (my thesis advisor and one of the world's great dialogue facilitators) once held up a cup and asked, "What is this?"

I responded by saying, "A cup."

He smiled and said, "No! It is a chalice given to me by the gods, and should you drink its nectar, I would have to kill you!"

His point was clear. What we see as a cup in our culture may be seen as a religious symbol in another.

In such exercises, Joe would then ask, "Could we engage in another person's meaning for a while?"

The anthropologist in me would say, "I can do that."

Then he would lead us through a variety of exercises that would help us engage in each other's meaning, reminding us that, in dialogue (among other forms of communication), everything is attached to a contextual meaning.

When I speak, I find it helpful to try to understand, to the best of my ability, my own assumptions and opinions. When I listen, I suspend my assumptions for a while. Try it. You don't need to believe in the speaker's beliefs when you are listening, but see if you can engage in his or her meaning. Joe had us practice this. He asked us to engage in the meaning of a powerful leader, a disenfranchised person, or a racist. Although I found this difficult, especially when asked to engage in the meaning of a racist by judging someone by the color of their skin, I also found it useful.

Bohm calls this act of engaging in another's meaning "suspending opinion."

It's not easy. If we interpret everything someone says through our meaning, we cannot actually hear what the speaker is saying. Instead we can only hear what we *think* he or she is saying. Basically, if we hear what we think someone is saying, we are really just hearing ourselves.

Suspending assumptions for a while can also help us overcome our belief in what we think is necessary for a meaningful conversation.

For instance, I used to think that speaking deeply with someone required us to possess the same values. Some of my university colleagues were military officers. As a pacifist, I questioned our ability to communicate about peace or peacekeeping. I assumed that only pacifists could really talk about peace. However, although my colleagues from the military had a different perspective, they taught me a lot about peacekeeping. Entering into a conversation with them led me to correspond with officers on a peacekeeping mission in Somalia, allowing me to hear, "on the ground," what peacemakers in the military really do. What a wonderful gift curiosity can be!

Such assumptions can be found any and everywhere. For example, someone living in poverty may believe that only impoverished people can really understand what it is like to live in poor conditions. This knee-jerk belief that like minds are necessary for dialogue can hinder our ability to listen to and learn from others. So I have tried to replace my assumptions with "curiosities." Differing perspectives and curious questions can create a wonderful conversation.

When engaging in community conversations, I often address this topic of suspending assumptions, even if this means having everyone take a few minutes to share with each other what it means to have a conversation. Using the dialogue techniques described in Part II of this book can also help people suspend assumption and meaning.

Many of us often try to find new ways to engage with each other, which will allow us to open up and be authentic. By suspending our assumptions and walking in each other's shoes, we can move from competing to win an argument, to expressing our ideas as a way to learn together, and in so doing to engage in true conversation.

Conversation and Engagement

The goal is really to create a conversation that helps people to think together.

— David Bohm, *On Dialogue*

Imagine a group of people thinking together. One person has an idea, someone else builds on that idea, and another person adds to that idea. The thoughts flow within the group rather than degenerating into people trying to convince one another of the rightness of their views. The original idea grows and so, too, do the possibilities.

The natural flow of conversations is essential to great community conversations, and it is what leads us to common understanding and commitment.

Understanding what conversation is and learning the techniques for better conversations helps us understand the importance of building trust between people. Trust helps us suspend judgment, find new opportunities, and explore possibilities for our communities together.

Conversation also leads to engagement. The time we spend together to build common understanding and a common vision commits us to the outcome and builds a sense of joint ownership for the work ahead of us.

2

ENGAGING

Community engagement means
people working collaboratively,
through inspired action and
learning, to create and realize
bold visions for their
common future.

~ Based on Tamarack's
mission statement

E ngagement — another building block of community conversations — is the incredible gift that only community conversations, built on trust and listening, can give us. When people get used to thinking together, they build the foundation for working together. They are engaged and share a common purpose and commitment to the outcome.

I experienced a profound shift in engagement with a leader in a community where I was working. It all started with a conversation.

Frank had recently joined the United Way in our area as executive director. We had not had much success in collaborating with the organization and saw a change in leadership as a good opportunity to engage them. Frank had a passion for community and brought a wonderfully innovative spirit to his work.

The engagement process started with a series of one-on-one conversations with him, which led to our inviting him to join a variety of community conversations that we were holding. Frank saw these conversations as a good way to get to know people from all sectors of the community.

I could see the change in Frank from one conversation to the next. The group's ideas and passion slowly began to resonate with him, and he started to trust the people and process of the conversation. Beginning to dream, Frank wondered how the goals of collaboration and the United Way's goals might complement each other. He became increasingly engaged. He even invited us to speak with his board about the work we were planning.

One day, after a particularly powerful conversation, Frank expressed excitement about the day and thanked me for inviting him. As we walked together to the parking lot, he asked, "Paul, can we have lunch soon? I have an idea that I would like to share with you."

Two months later, Frank launched a citywide campaign, working with his donor businesses to consider how to move two hundred families out of poverty. Then he raised enough money to hire someone to assist a few of the member agencies in creating a social enterprise to find jobs for low-income families.

Frank became engaged because we were engaged in a *real* conversation. He had practical work to get done and saw, through deliberate community conversations, that our roundtable of multi-sector leaders could advance his efforts. We were there to *Listen!* and support him.

Once people engage in the ideas of others and experience authentic and passionate conversation, they begin to move from talking to *doing*. "What can I do?" they ask. "How can I contribute to this remarkable conversation?"

And that sets up some important expectations.

Expectations Flow from Engagement

"Why ask if you do not plan on doing anything about it?"
— A participant at a government consultation

Listening to others, entering into their meaning, and joining creative energies to dream of real solutions leads to engagement: the shared commitment to find and implement decisions. Why does this happen? Because as community conversations lead to expectations, they engage people at a deep level.

A mentor once gave me the gift of this wise advice: "If you are not prepared to do anything about it, do not ask your community, 'What needs to be done?' "

In other words, if you are part of an organization, government, or a collaboration of organizations seeking community input, it's important for you to recognize that community conversations spark expectations.

I learned this first-hand when engaging in dialogue with a leadership roundtable.

Mary was an incredible volunteer. She was a low-income single parent who had become a member of this roundtable because she wanted to help those "who were once like me."

She enjoyed the conversations and saw the merits of getting to the root of the poverty issue in our community. She understood that conversations could deepen commitment and heighten trust across sectors.

But Mary grew impatient. One day, out of frustration, she said, "I know we need to talk, and I know that building trust takes time, but let's get on with it! When are we going to change things?"

As a leadership roundtable, we took this to heart. We felt that Mary was expressing the views of more than one person.

We began two processes to address Mary's concern.

The first process was to document the changes that individuals had made as a result of the conversations. When we did this, we saw the tremendous influence of the people who were part of our leadership roundtable. We found that they were changing and learning from the conversations they attended with us.

The second was to consider short-term or "quick win" activities that we could tackle together. We knew that these would not address root problems. But we also knew that tackling these issues would help us exercise collective knowledge and power. This process felt like practice for the work we knew was to come.

Since *Listening!* creates expectations for action, you might want to consider the following ideas when you are involved in community conversations.

- Ask, "Who will affect the system? Who can contribute to or benefit from the solution?" The answers to these questions will tell you who should be part of the conversation. If we open the conversation to anyone, we run the risk of creating expectations for groups of people who do not have the influence to bring about change. Consider the energy and capacity of the people and groups involved in order to maximize your efficiency. Be strategic when considering those to invite to your conversation. (See chapter 7, on the Top 100 Partners Exercise conversation technique.)

- Recognize that power can be formal, informal, positional, or by association. Engage a broad range of opinions in order to represent the system you desire to change.

- Use dialogue techniques so people can hear many points of view.

- Ask questions that help people reflect on what they want changed and how they need to change. Examples might be, "Describe a community in which poverty could not exist. How would people live in this community and with each other? Why don't we live this way now?"

- Remember, we need people to be engaged and to bring what they can to the process. Ask people what they are able to contribute to the change they would like to see. Time? Money? Resources?

- Take the necessary time to find a path forward. Help people recognize that this is a journey and their voice is important. The journey's dynamic shouldn't be "What will you do for me?" It should be "What can we do together?"

Whether you are building a collaboration of some sort or trying to gain insights for making policy changes, there are two things that remain true: When holding any type of community conversation, it's important for you to consider the people in the room and the questions that are being asked. The people you bring together and what you ask them will always create expectations among them, no matter what the purpose of the conversation may be.

Multi-sector Engagement

I cannot get to a place of unknowing by myself or with those who think like I do. But it is to that place of unknowing that I need to go if I am ever to know.
— Paul Born during an ever-so-brief moment of wisdom

For most of us, our first thought, when planning a community conversation about an issue we hope to address, is to invite people who already agree with us. This is especially true at the beginning of such conversations. Given how difficult it is to suspend assumptions, we may think that if we want to talk about poverty, we should bring together organizations dedicated to fighting poverty, or that if we want to talk about crime prevention, we should gather groups dedicated to building safe communities. We believe that bringing the like-minded together will allow us to form a solid foundation on which to build in more diversity over time.

This has not been my experience, however. On the tour mentioned above with Surrey's social agencies, we heard one side of the community's story. When we visited Surrey's business community, we heard another side. It wasn't until we brought these two seemingly disparate sides together that the full story about the community began to emerge.

I have worked with hundreds of single- and multi-sector groups. For years I have tried to understand the dynamic that occurs when we bring together the various sectors in a community.

Single-sector groups are where most of us spend the majority of our time: business people with business people; social agencies with social agencies; government officials with government officials; activists with activists.

Multi-sector groups are formed when a variety of groups, such as business, government, and volunteer groups, work together, think together, and learn together with the people who are being directly affected by the issue they are trying to address, whether these be the poor or those affected by an environmental issue, gangs, or increased crime.

Single-sector groups are more prone to:

- Define the problem.
- Seek solutions to problems.
- Seek to convince and to show that their solution to the problem is the most effective.
- Assume that their purpose and core service values are the same.

Multi-sector groups are prone to:

- Tell stories.
- Define and isolate the issues that make up the problem.
- Seek to understand the other sectors' point of view.

- See conversation as an opportunity to learn.
- Suspend their expertise. Members of the group may ask, "Am I qualified to be in this conversation?"
- Suspend assumptions. Group members are brought out of their comfort zone and asked to enter into conversation with people they normally do not engage with in dialogue.

I recommend holding community conversations with as many different sectors present as possible. The simple act of holding a multi-sector conversation can help people suspend assumptions and move together into a space of unknowing.

Why do I say "a space of unknowing"?

Jim was a high-level banker, Nancy was a single mother, Frank worked for a social agency. They came to a community conversation and after the first meeting they all said the same thing: "I don't feel qualified to be here. Are you sure I'm the right person?"

Jim said he knew about business, not poverty.

Nancy felt out of place among so many influential leaders.

Frank was touched by how unusual — how honest — the conversation was.

I often hear these types of comments in multi-sector conversations, when highly qualified people move into a different place. This place of *unknowing* is exactly where we want the conversation to begin. It is where people tell stories, open up to learning, and listen to one another. A wonderful place to be.

Multi-sector conversations bridge the silos between government, business, and the voluntary sector and give unique voice to the people affected by the issue. This diversity makes conversations much more productive.

Multi-sector conversations also harness the unique skills and contributions of each sector. As business talks to the voluntary sector and as government talks to people in poverty, they understand better the unique roles and skills and resources that each sector brings. These skills and resources are the assets of the community. When they are harnessed and brought into harmony, the sum is greater than the individual parts.

Multi-sector conversations also link power systems. Business, government, and advocacy groups each possess the power to make things happen. By linking this power and agreeing on a desired change, the power of each sector is multiplied. Multi-sector consensus on community issues is rare. In my experience, when it happens, ideas turn to action quickly and resources are found to realize the dream.

Most importantly, multi-sector conversations provide the platform to understand that even though we all want the best for our community, and even though we have a common vision of what our community should be, agreement on how we go about making it that way need not be the same. Each sector has unique gifts and these can be exercised toward realizing the vision. In this way, community conversations provide, first, a forum for learning from each other and, second, a forum for compromising with each other. A forum to get to a joint solution — one in which we all agree broadly on what we want to accomplish and can embrace one another's contributions to getting there. A forum to understand that a common vision does not necessarily require a common approach.

Our communities need to have the kinds of conversations that foster deep trust between sectors. We all live in a community and we all benefit or are hurt by the actions of any one sector of our community. Talking together as different sectors helps us see and understand how connected we really are.

Get the *Unusual* Suspects Together

Each word a person speaks is filled with meaning from the past, the present, and memories of the future. And, each time a person speaks a word, the meaning of that word changes somehow as it both creates and becomes part of everyday life. Words are rich with meaning. But meaning never stands still. It is always (as are people) unfolding through time.

— Joe Schaeffer

Even when we are being strategic about those to include in a community conversation, we can easily overlook people who can be very helpful. We need to be open to the unusual "stranger."

After I met with a group of community leaders several years ago, one of the individuals approached me with a check for $20,000. I was surprised and very pleased, but somehow mustered up the courage to ask, "Why, when you have heard me speak for only a few short minutes, would you give me so much money?" He responded by saying that he liked what he had heard and tended to make decisions quickly.

This man was a not-so-well-known entrepreneur who attended the meeting at a friend's request. Uncomfortable accepting money from someone who knew very little about our work, I returned his check and said, "I'll make a deal with you. If you spend a day with me learning more about our work and sharing your story, I will accept the money."

The man agreed. Within a year he was chairing our unique collaboration and over time donated $200,000 to our work. More valuable than this man's money was his involvement in our work. He intuitively understood our goals and believed deeply in multi-sector collaboration for poverty reduction. With his help we opened doors to a wide range of community people we otherwise would have never encountered. He invited me to political gatherings that I thought I would never want to support. He convened a round-table of people with unique perspectives. He had access to power that I didn't even know about.

I have been profoundly affected by this experience. Every call, every inquiry, regardless of how "out of the ordinary," has become extremely important to me.

Who are the strangers and how can they help? They may appear as a homeless person on the street, someone with a disability, or an unusually entrepreneurial government bureaucrat. I am not sure that the "stranger" is someone you can automatically think of when you brainstorm who might join a conversation. However, as you open yourself up to new ideas and new people, a natural curiosity will emerge. Ordinary stories will become extraordinary; people without technical expertise will be seen to have tremendous wisdom; people who seem not to care will reveal a deep commitment to helping others.

Community conversations open us to journeys of others and ask us to reveal our own journey. I cannot fully explain how or even why this works, but I do know this: It happens every time.

Expect it to happen. Be ready to invite these unusual suspects into your conversation.

The Dynamics of Power

Everybody knows the fight was fixed
The poor stay poor and the rich get rich
That's how it goes
Everybody knows

— Leonard Cohen

The issues and dynamics of power often arise when a community conversation between people from various sectors is convened. The question often asked is, "How can people with such different power relationships really talk with each other?"

The power relationship for some may be between a welfare officer and a welfare recipient, a boss and an employee, a funder and a grant recipient. Others may see the power relationship as gender or race related.

A collaboration I was involved in had been meeting for almost a year, during which time we had reached out to all sectors in the community. We even had three low-income representatives on our leadership roundtable. However, despite our efforts, our collaboration was not working.

The community conversations were great, but the dynamic within our leadership team was not progressing. Our low-income representatives were not speaking as much as we had hoped. When they did speak, it was always followed by a moment of silence from other members.

We decided to have a conversation to ask what was going on. Because we had built a fair bit of trust throughout the year, the conversation was open and frank.

The low-income representatives had spoken, often, from personal experience. This was their power (knowledge base), and it was welcomed by the group. But in this frank discussion, the others shared what they felt when they heard these stories.

"How do we respond to such personal stories?" a government representative asked.

"I feel so sad when I hear these stories," a participant from the business sector said.

The responses continued, with members of the collaborative generally expressing sympathy for our low-income participants and feeling guilty for not doing more.

I was perplexed. This honesty should have opened the members of our collaboration to one another. Instead, it was shutting us down.

After a lengthy conversation, we agreed on an experiment, one that would forever change how the roundtable acted.

The idea came from one of our business leaders.

He suggested that if we wanted to seriously consider the voices of the low-income participants, we must use their experiences as a lens. He suggested that we form an ongoing focus group, represented by the low-income leaders at our table. We set out with them to recruit more than fifty low-income people to meet monthly to discuss issues of relevance to the leadership roundtable. We agreed to refrain from making major decisions until they were shared with and processed by the focus group for their insights. These insights would then be shared with the leadership roundtable by our low-income representatives.

This changed the power dynamic between members. Although we continued to share personal stories, leaders at the table now saw the low-income participants more as representatives of the focus group than as isolated individuals living in poverty.

This was not a perfect solution: It did not change the "true" power dynamic between those who had positional and financial power and those who did not. But it did change the dynamic of the conversations and increased the effectiveness of our work together.

There is no easy solution to the question of power and engagement. It is important in these situations to consider justice, stereotypes, and power dynamics, and be open to experimenting with solutions.

Here are a few ideas to consider:

- Ensure that there are multiple voices present from vulnerable populations. If you include low-income people, make sure that at least three or four are in the room. Give them an opportunity to converse with one another in order to build trust and support.

- Ensure that your group has a solid understanding of effective dialogue and the importance of suspending assumptions. Then talk openly about power.

- Consider creating a "reference group" for those who come to the table without positional power. By creating a reference group of fifty low-income individuals who met monthly with the four low-income leaders who sat on our leadership roundtable, we were able to change the relationship between the members of the roundtable. When these four leaders came to the table, they spoke with authority and power, representing a very significant voice in our poverty-reduction initiative.

- Open people up by exploring how power is also a matter of framing ideas, addressing perspectives, and recognizing that there are people in the room who have power over others.

- Recognize that power issues cannot be overcome by everyone. Sometimes it is better to change the dynamic by asking people who cannot work with those who have power over them to leave the roundtable. Similarly, if there are people who consistently use their power inappropriately, ask them to step aside for the good of the whole.

Rely on Human Goodness

Courageous acts aren't done by people who believe in human badness. Why risk anything if we don't believe in each other? Why stand up for anyone if we don't believe they're worth saving? Who you think I am will determine what you're willing to do on my behalf...
— Margaret Wheatley, "Relying on Human Goodness"

Margaret Wheatley is one of my favorite writers. She has a way of describing, with poetry and grace, exactly what I feel. She often conveys the tension between hope and despair, optimism and cynicism, fear and faith. The quote above, taken from a newspaper article she wrote, describes the "lens" that opens us to seeing and engaging with others. This belief in people leads us to conversation about the things that matter to us. Wheatley goes on to say that the first value of such conversations is, "We rely on human goodness."

> *In conversations even with strangers, we assume they want from their life what we do from ours: a chance to help others, to learn, to be recognized, to find meaning.*

She says that the second value is, "We assume good intent."

Relying on human goodness requires more than suspending assumptions or necessities. It is at the root of our belief system. It challenges us to think about others' intent because we hope they will think about our intent, too.

By recognizing good intentions, we have the opportunity for a new type of conversation. In her keynote address "Turning to One Another," Wheatley writes:

> *In most organizations, we are trained to ask, "What's wrong?" and "How can we fix it?" This is a demoralizing process, and a typical one. Instead, [we can] learn to ask two very different questions: "What's possible here?" and "Who cares?"*
>
> *When we ask "Who cares?" we invite in others who are also passionate about an issue. And, when we ask "What's possible?" it opens us up to unprecedented creativity.*

When we start a conversation by asking, "What's wrong and how can we fix it?" we spark criticism, and not necessarily of the healthy sort. The mood in a room can quickly move to blame and anger. We focus on isolating the problem and, in turn, quickly believe we can fix it. My experience is that these conversations are seldom hopeful or helpful. They lack creativity and often break down because people begin to feel despair.

When we ask questions like, "Who cares and what is possible?" we immediately open ourselves to one another. These questions cause us to reach out and engage. By asking these questions, we are also admitting that the solution is not necessarily ours alone to fix and that the solution may take some time to realize. We recognize that the conversation itself is a big part of the solution.

A "relying on human goodness" lens is profoundly important when holding community dialogues. When we invite others into a conversation, our basic belief should be that they do care. This belief will allow us to seek what is possible, not what is impossible. Can any other route provide this opportunity? Can we seek "possibility" with people who do not care?

Believing that people care and seeking possibilities with them makes conversation productive. It opens up a space for creativity to flourish within and between us. In creating this space, we allow thoughts to flow with the conversation, rather than causing it to degenerate into tugs of war between people who are trying to convince each other. As the conversation grows, so does trust, and so does the commitment to realize the possibilities to effect positive change.

In such conversations, people cease to be combatants in favor of becoming collaborators.

3

COLLABORATING

We are caught in an inescapable
network of mutuality, tied in a
single garment of destiny.
Whatever affects one directly,
affects all directly.

~ Martin Luther King Jr.

We often use jargon to describe simple acts. Community conversations that engage people in collaboration can be conducted in a jargon-free zone. These conversations are common and can be fairly simple. When asked to describe the purpose of a community conversation, I often refer to it as people talking with one another (planning), agreeing to work together (partnering), and doing something (projects) in order to get something done (performance).

An everyday example of conversations leading to collaboration can be found at the dinner table.

As we're eating together, someone says, "Hey, let's do something this weekend." Ideas are shared (planning) and a sense of wanting to do something together (partnering) emerges. "Let's go for a hike and a picnic." Everyone agrees that this is a great idea (the project). The rest of the conversation is about the details of the outing with everyone contributing their ideas in order to ensure a good time for all (performance).

Building Collaborative Communities

The collaborative premise says: If you bring the appropriate people together in constructive ways with good information, they will create authentic visions and strategies for addressing the shared concerns of the organization and community.

— David Chrislip

Community conversations are about engaging community members in a dialogue that mobilizes the collective energy of a community. As for how we engage our community to achieve this collective energy — it depends.

Engagement depends on community conditions and the strength of the organizing group. If there is a strong history of collaboration, this process is most often quick and can take place in larger groups. If the credibility of the organizing group is weak or involves a single sector, more strategic and smaller meetings may be needed. The key is to assess the readiness of the community to move from an idea to planning. You cannot rush this stage. A few ideas may sprout, but your chances of success are greatly diminished if you move too quickly from visioning to planning.

Assessing the type of dialogue needed in the early stages of a collaboration is helped by considering the history of collaboration in a community, the public perception of the people who make up the collaboration, and the social and political framing of the idea you are collaborating to effect. This will enable a collaboration to realize who should be part of the conversation in order for the collaboration to have the credibility to effect change.

If a community does not have a strong history of collaborating, then its members need to learn more about collaboration and its barriers in their community. They need to take a careful look at the issue. If it is not framed within a context that is important to or resonates with the residents of the community, it would be wise for them to reframe the issue. Taking stock of these factors early on may be the difference between success and failure.

A Few Tips

- If you are part of a single-sector group that wishes to include other sectors, look for people who can bridge the sectors rather than trying to "just find anyone." If you are in the business community and want to build a bridge to the voluntary sector, consider asking people in your group if they volunteer on any voluntary sector boards, or have neighbors from that sector.

- Engage a leader with influence. Influence is different from power. A person with influence has the power to convene. I start by asking, "Do we have the right person? If this person invited ten leaders from their sector to our meeting, would the majority of them show up?"

- Building a collaborative around a good idea requires leadership and strategy. I define leadership as having a vision of the future and doing what it takes to realize that vision. When you convene the conversation, have you taken stock of your vision of what it is you want to change? What is your own passion for this change?

- The goal of collaboration is not to exercise power over others but to use the power of the collaborative to engage people with power. When we are in harmony and motivated by a vision, we naturally adapt to and accommodate the desired change. Change often starts slowly but then accelerates quickly.

- The power of a community conversation is that it fosters collaboration and, in turn, helps a community project a unified front. Funders are much more interested in learning and in providing resources to address community issues when various sectors of a collaboration speak with one voice.

Community conversations lead to collaboration if we engage the right people in synch with the right vision. Over time, the vision is held in common, and the people in conversation engage with one another to create the change they desire to see.

I spent a dozen years building the Community Opportunities Development Association (CODA) in Cambridge, Ontario. During my tenure, CODA helped more than 5,500 people get back to work and nearly 1,200 unemployed people start small businesses.

During that time I often made community presentations with the City's business commissioner. He often started his presentation by tossing golf balls into the audience, claiming that his job was to play a lot of golf in order to sell municipal land and attract new business into the area. He then introduced me by saying, "This man represents Cambridge's other economic development department," going on to explain that CODA existed to help the twenty percent of our community's residents who had the lowest income. I always thought this was a good way to describe what we did.

CODA became one of the country's largest and most successful community economic development organizations with a staff of eighty people and massive community support in a vibrant, progressive city. However, I was perplexed by our community's continuing poverty, despite the recognition and relative success of our programs. No matter how many people we helped or how effectively we helped them, we could not make a dent in our community's impoverished conditions.

The elevating statistics compelled me to ask, "What if we worked in a different way?" A group of us began to talk about community building rather than helping the unemployed. Instead of focusing our efforts on helping people find jobs, we worked together, using collaborative approaches, to build our community. This shift in focus began to make the kind of difference we had always hoped for.

CODA started several new community-building programs. Opportunities Planning was one of them. As part of the program, we hired residents living in our community's nineteen low-income neighborhoods and trained them to help their neighbors find jobs. This work grew into a Millennium campaign that rallied our community, forming a large multi-sector collaboration toward a formidable goal of reducing poverty in our region to the lowest in Canada. Two years later, these programs were recognized by the United Nations and received a number of provincial and national awards.

Today, our city — and, indeed, the entire region — reflect a vibrant community that enjoys one of the lowest, if not *the* lowest, poverty rate in the country: the only city in the country to eliminate concentrated or neighborhood-based poverty. We reached this milestone as a community by talking together across sectors, working together without judgment, and thinking differently about how to help those in need.

Community leaders are increasingly recognizing that transactional services, while important, cannot solve the complex problems facing our communities and their most vulnerable residents. People at risk often face a multitude of issues — some of which might be personal, while others might be situational, such as a community's quality of neighborhoods, economic health, and attitude toward racism or indifference.

The drive toward better, more comprehensive solutions to complex issues is epitomized by the phenomenon known as Comprehensive Community Initiatives (CCIs). CCIs work across sectoral boundaries because they recognize that complex issues, such as racism and poverty, can be addressed only if problems and solutions are aligned.

Communities are collaborating to find a new way to harness everyone's passion and energy and bring these into harmony around a new vision. Over time, communities change as citizens learn to work together. This is the miracle of collaborations powered by community conversations.

How Collaboration Works

For those who have seen the Earth from space, and for the hundreds and perhaps thousands more who will, the experience most certainly changes your perspective. The things that we share in our world are far more valuable than those which divide us.

— Donald Williams

The Five Phases of Collaboration

I have learned about and observed more than 300 collaborations. None of them works the same! Though it is difficult to recognize similar patterns within any collaboration, we have identified five phases that occur in a collaborative cycle. While the delineation of these

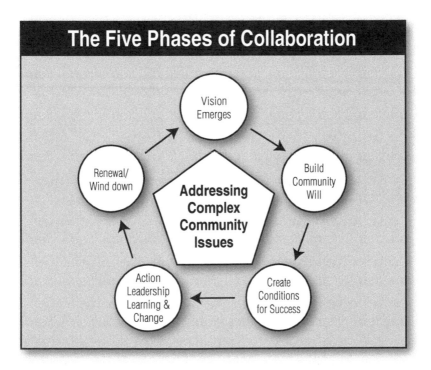

The Five Phases of Collaboration

Vision Emerges

Build Community Will

Addressing Complex Community Issues

Renewal/ Wind down

Create Conditions for Success

Action Leadership Learning & Change

phases as shown in the diagram is not perfect, many have found it helpful when thinking about the way they work.

As we have discussed earlier in this book, collaboration is the critical ingredient in addressing complex community issues in order to develop comprehensive community initiatives. The five development phases described here are patterns that we have observed, ones that we know can help groups determine what stage of a collaborative cycle they are in.

In Phase One, a vision emerges. An example of this occurs when a small group of people start to talk about advancing a community issue, such as reducing poverty or crime. They sense that something needs to change and that the old system of organizing is not making any progress on the issue.

Through conversation, they:

- Embrace the idea that the whole community needs to be involved.
- Take stock of community assets.
- Identify people and issues that need to be addressed and begin to broaden their conversation to include them.
- Articulate and share their early vision with the community.

Phase Two leads the group to reach out and build community will. For example, as people in the collaboration see that their vision resonates with others, they begin to reach out to a broader constituency. This phase often lasts longer than a year. The smaller leadership team often uses dialogue tools to facilitate conversation with representatives from many stakeholder groups.

Together, they:

- Become more deliberate about multi-sector engagement.
- Begin to develop a common understanding of an issue that is broadly shared.
- Articulate the issue and possible solutions.
- Become progressive in their thinking, opening themselves to new possibilities and innovation.
- Continuously communicate to and engage with the rest of the community.

Phase Three emerges from Phase Two and occurs, most often, when people are ready to move into the "doing" stage of the work. This is the time to build the conditions for success. At this point, people want to become more concrete about their activities. Working groups are formed to:

- Help individuals who are engaged to connect with the organizations they represent and to formalize their membership in the collaboration. This involves moving membership from individual to organizational. It is important to develop a membership at this stage.
- Develop a formal community plan for action.
- Secure sufficient financial and technical resources.
- Establish an appropriate leadership and governance structure to steward the next phase of work.

Phase Four, described as the action-learning-leadership-change phase, occurs when the group is ready to implement their plan. This does not mean that they have been waiting for this phase to act. A tremendous amount of informal and even smaller formal activities usually take place in the second and third phases. However, in this phase the group works together to implement the original strategies and initiatives, adapting them as they unfold.

Broadly speaking, the collaboration takes on a mix of or all of these tasks:

- **Raising public awareness of the issue.**
    - Building a media profile.
    - Hosting public events and distributing "issue" materials.

- **Forming a strategic focus in the community to effectively impact the issue.**
    - Networking and sharing information between members.
    - Researching the issue to understand and identify its root causes.
    - Planning with partners to implement strategic changes and launch projects.

- **Supporting local action.**
    - Lobbying and advocacy activities.
    - Improving access to funding.
    - Creating social marketing targeted to specific change strategies.
    - Providing technical assistance and coaching to member organizations that are undertaking change strategies.
    - Brokering and facilitating relationships between members, and bridging power relationships.
    - Peer learning.
    - Managing programs and services.

The final phase, Phase Five, is the renewal or wind down of the initiative. While Phase Four can last for several years, the leadership structure will eventually need to be reviewed, and a new plan may be required to advance the work. Some collaborations find that this is a good opportunity to wind down the initiative and begin the process of working on another issue. Communities involved in this phase often reflect on their experience and determine whether they have accomplished all that they can or whether they need to renew their effort with new leadership, direction, organization, and resources.

In this phase, groups will typically:

- Assess the energy and commitment of the members and determine if and for how long their work should continue.
- Engage in a summative evaluation. This can help a group see how much they have impacted a community over the years they have worked together.
- Assess their leadership team.
- Consider the origins of their work. A process of letting go of projects and ideas and a birthing of new projects and ideas may occur.

It's important to recognize that these five phases are a construct that helps us place our work into a continuum of activities. Our work does not always progress cleanly from one phase to the next. Progress can be "messy," but the construct of these five phases can help people assess the state of their work. I often ask, "What phase do you feel your collaborative is in?"

Act Like an Organization, Think Like a Movement

In addition to the Five Phases of Collaboration, we have observed a process that overrides, or at least dominates, the time and energy of the collaboration through each of the five phases. The groups that do this well have more success both in implementing project ideas and in achieving large-scale systems change.

We call this process *acting like an organization* (moving through the five phases of development with skill) and *thinking like a movement* (acting in a way that builds engagement, purpose, and momentum), in order to build a movement for change to become the communities we want to be.

When thinking like a movement, the emphasis is more on the *way* we do the work than on the content of the work. The process itself is important. This is exactly why the role of community conversations is so critical to the success of large-scale collaborations. Every event and every conversation becomes an opportunity for engagement, and every opportunity for engagement becomes an opportunity to talk about the values and the vision and purpose behind the work. The desire is to create the conditions that will stimulate the momentum of the collective. Thinking like a movement is the pursuit of larger systems change.

As you will see in the diagram below, we have observed three distinct but interrelated stages involved in thinking like a movement. They are:

1. Working in a way that builds engagement.
2. Working in a way that builds purpose.
3. Working in a way that builds momentum.

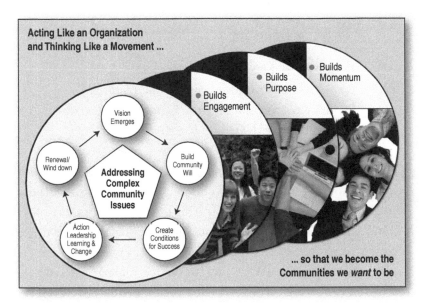

Building Engagement. The overall work is to engage the right people when you work and learn. The goal of your collaborative should be to build a continuous cycle of people talking with one another, agreeing to work together, creating ideas together, and then working together to ensure that these ideas achieve their intended result.

We often start a collaborative conversation with a small core of committed people. We ground this group in our way of being through dialogue. However, given our desire for system change, we broaden engagement and use every opportunity to introduce the right people to the change we are pursuing.

Given that we have limited energy and resources, this work must be strategic. We know that we must engage in a conversation with multiple sectors and voices at the table. The challenge is to engage people in new ideas, leading them toward their highest aspirations.

- **Working in a way that builds engagement means that we must:**
  - Engage the right people (multi-sector).
  - Facilitate conversations (learning and planning).
  - Facilitate the agreement to work together (clusters).
  - Build and implement ideas together.

Building Purpose. Engaging people is one thing, but simply having a group of people excited about working together is not going to get a collaborative very far. This is why allocating time for a community to talk is so important, and why bringing multiple sectors to the table is equally important. Hosting learning opportunities, bringing in speakers, and producing materials is critical at this stage. However, it is important not to be in a rush to agree on the vision.

When groups are involved in purpose building, they must also consider the collective nature of the work. They must understand that sustained engagement requires people to feel that they belong to a community of people working together. Time must be taken in purpose building to care about the people you are engaging: This means celebrating together, monitoring involvement, and making it personal. *People* are doing this work.

- **Work in a way that builds purpose and:**
  - Gives time for an idea to become an aspiration.
  - Develops a vision that resonates broadly.
  - Celebrates working together on behalf of others.
  - Uses every opportunity to engage the community and to build momentum toward a movement for change.

Building Momentum. Momentum is something that people feel when they are engaged. They start to talk about the work differently. They start to change behaviors. And they show up! What is being built here is a continuous cycle of collaboration.

Momentum is also something that we can measure through the number of people in our database, the number of people who come to meetings, the number of new ideas being acted upon, the number of people from each sector and from varying levels of the each organization, the amount of change we have seen in the system, the capacity to work differently in organizations and people, and, most importantly, the number of people whose lives have improved because of our work.

It is important, as people talk, agree, and design, that the system becomes *relentless*. Only people engaged in their highest aspiration create this characteristic.

- **Engage in a way that builds momentum. To do this, it must be remembered that:**
  - Building credibility intensifies momentum.
    - Engage with cornerstone people and multi-sector institutions.
    - Communicate the story as if the change you want to see is occurring.

  - Building capacity sustains momentum.
    - Learn to work together better.
    - Learn how to do the work better.
    - Watch for fear!

- ◦ Building capital fuels momentum. Always be aware that:
    - The need for money grows as momentum grows.
    - Donors should be engaged early.
    - Money and power are interrelated.

Recognizing and Harnessing Community Assets

Bring what you've got.
Put it in the pot.
Every bit counts from the largest to the least.
Together we can celebrate a stone soup feast.
— "Stone Soup" as told by Heather Forest

Music fans around the world are familiar with the rich and powerful voice of Italian tenor Andrea Bocelli. His ability to interpret all forms of music, from popular ballads to arias, has endeared him to people throughout the world. What some may not know is that this incredible musician is blind.

Imagine if we were to think of Bocelli not for his incredible musical abilities, but for his inability to see. If we focused on his blindness, we would miss out on hearing his romantic tenor voice and feeling the emotional empathy that he brings to all of his music. When we hear his voice — the depth and clarity, the passion and joy — we forget about his disability. We are transformed by the beauty of his voice.

Communities are complex. They often experience real and desperate interrelated challenges. But they are also places of richness and caring. When we see the assets of a community, we can put its challenges into perspective and harness its strengths to make it even better. Community assets are rooted in people, their dreams, their leadership, their hope. Assets include government, health, religious, and educational institutions; caring businesses and community organizations; and the general acts of compassionate citizens and civic responses already present in the community.

In most communities in developed countries, the majority of residents live in quality housing, have stable jobs, and are members of functional families. Many of them donate and volunteer. Most desire to build a better quality of life for themselves, their families, and generally for their community. Our challenge is not finding people who care; it is engaging them in active caring.

Simply put, people who care are a community's greatest asset. By working together, they can bring about real change. By bringing them into a conversation, we can turn the collective hopelessness we often feel about homelessness, crime, youth pregnancy, and low civic engagement into a shared hope for change.

Our perception of our community and its assets is important. It shapes how we get involved, our understanding of what is possible, our dreams, and the role our organization has in fulfilling those dreams. Our perception also shapes the types of dialogues we want to have with people.

How Can Conversation Help Us Consider Our Community Assets?

Start every conversation by reminding yourself of your community's positive qualities. This builds commitment and energy among the conversation's participants.

Recognizing community assets brings the best out of people and encourages a positive spirit. Sustainable, intrinsic change rarely comes from people who are shamed into doing something.

A dialogue between people who have been identified as assets to a community is much more productive than one convened between people who are identified as the problem.

Just like a spoonful of sugar helps the medicine go down, seeing people as community assets makes difficult conversations easier.

Change is much easier when it builds on an organization's strengths. For example, by helping a business understand how it already contributes to community building, the conversation about what *more* it can do comes with ease.

(It would be helpful for you to revisit this chapter before you read about the Top 100 Partners Exercise later in this book.)

Collaboration Creates Harmony

Harmony: A combination of notes that are sung or played at the same time providing momentum and richness to melody.
— Encarta Dictionary

The Orpheus Orchestra is a Grammy-award-winning chamber orchestra. It is based in New York City and has been thrilling music lovers on four continents for over thirty years. It is also a self-governing organization that performs without a conductor. As the

New York Times has written, "It is worth paying attention to almost anything these conductor-less players put their collective hand, mind and heart to." Central to the orchestra's distinctive personality is its unique practice of sharing and rotating leadership roles.

According to members of the orchestra, they organized themselves without a conductor not because "something was broken" but because they wanted to make *great* music as opposed to *good* music. Working collaboratively, they have created unique interpretations and have organized in a way that requires them to deliberately listen to one another in order to encourage the very best from everyone in the orchestra.

So often in community work we begin with the premise that we have to fix a system that is broken. What if we suspended this judgment about the brokenness of our communities for a while? What if we could believe that our communities have tremendous assets and resources and loads of untapped talent? Would we think differently about how we might organize ourselves to harness these resources?

What if, like the Orpheus Orchestra, we started from the premise that we all have talent and energy and we should consider a new way of organizing in order bring out the best in all of us?

The premise of improving rather than fixing our communities begs for a new approach. It requires us to introduce new methodologies and new disciplines that take us to another level. This is why we collaborate. It is our desire to create a new system for organizing ourselves.

Organizing ourselves for collaboration requires us to bring assets, especially people in organizations, into harmony. By seeing caring and talented people in our community and bringing them together — to collaborate and harness the best they have to offer in order to effect change — we begin the process of refining the systems and disciplines that already make us good. A new way of working together emerges. Collaboration is this new way.

How Do We Begin a Conversation That Helps Us Work in Harmony?

Consider the following suggestions to help your collaboration work in harmony. When beginning a conversation:

- Ask, "How do we get from good to better?" instead of asking, "What are the problems facing our community and who is to blame?"

- Consider how you would work differently if you wanted to improve things rather than fix them.

- Ask, "Is our current system working in harmony? If so, how? If not, how can we improve our collaboration?"

- Host a conversation about collaboration. Ask, "What is it? How have others collaborated successfully?" Then ask, "What should we do together?"

4

CASTING A VISION

The transformational leader
also understands the power
of vision, especially when a
community requires revitalization
and change. It is usually the vision
which gives a community the
energy to embark on the change
and for the participants affected
by the changes to believe such
change is worthwhile.

~ Paul Born, from paper
"Leadership as Energy"

The melodic cooing of a newborn child can melt any heart. When a baby enters "the family system," it causes each member of the family to change. A woman becomes a mother, a man becomes a father, a couple becomes parents, parents become grandparents, and siblings become aunts and uncles. Our natural response in all of these changing relationships is to engage.

A Compelling Vision

Cherish your visions and your dreams, as they are the children of your soul, the blueprints of your ultimate achievements.

— Napoleon Hill

Imagine if we were able to create a vision that compelled our community system to change in the way a baby creates a family. This would not be just any vision, but a vision so compelling that it would capture the imagination and heart and innate desire of a whole community.

What role does conversation play in creating such a vision? How might we agree on a vision that is owned by the whole community? In conversation with all sectors of the community, we are able to frame our vision in such a way that it resonates with people from businesses, the voluntary sector and, most importantly, those who are served by the vision.

Framing our collaborative response is an important part of building multi-sector collaboration. Holding effective community conversations can help us to do this. We are able to listen to members of a collaborative as they talk about their vision for the kind of community they want and then translate these into words that resonate with the whole group.

A good idea in its formative stages is seldom expressed in a way that resonates deeply with a whole community. All communities are different and unique, so it is important to frame the idea within the conditions or climate of the community. In other words, what resonates in one community might not resonate in another. It is only in sharing the idea with many people and hearing which aspects of the idea resonate with them that we will be able to frame the idea in a way that has broad appeal.

I have learned this by framing the work of poverty in several different countries.

The Region of Waterloo, Ontario, is one of the most dynamic and successful communities in Canada. Known as the country's Silicon Valley, Waterloo is home to two universities and one of the country's highest per-capita incomes and charitable giving rates, as well as its highest level of volunteerism.

Despite all of these assets, poverty remained constant in the region for nearly twenty years — ebbing and flowing with the economy, but seeing no real improvement overall. In 1996 I had the privilege of leading a dynamic group of volunteers to embark on a conversation to develop a unique Millennium goal. Our vision was to create the lowest level of poverty in the nation. To do this, we committed to moving two thousand families out of poverty by the year 2000.

After much conversation, we agreed that we did not want to have a negative conversation. The overwhelming responsibility of "solving" a problem that had been with us far too long had us feeling helpless. We agreed that we wanted a positive vision that might spark our imagination of what might be possible.

The vision we crafted together was called Opportunities 2000 (OP2000) and it was unique in several ways. It built on our community's pride (we are a very entrepreneurial community) and was embedded into our culture of caring. OP2000 also used the coming of a new millennium to motivate people, giving them a real and tangible goal. The rally that ensued was nothing short of miraculous. Can you envision a better way to usher in the new millennium than to be known for having the lowest level of poverty in the country?

One city has framed its poverty response as improving the quality of life for all citizens. Building on the commonly held belief that it already has the best quality of life in the country, they named their initiative the Quality of Life CHALLENGE. In doing so, they engaged the community in a conversation about what a good quality of life would be for the city's most vulnerable.

In a community with one of the highest per-capita poverty rates in the country, the issue is framed through a vision of being "average" — by reaching the national "average" poverty rate of fifteen percent from the city's twenty-eight percent poverty rate. This resonated with people in the community and was seen not only as a realistic but as an imperative goal.

A community with one of the highest child poverty rates in the nation framed its issue as being "the best place to raise a child." This came after nearly two years of talking and working together on the issue of poverty. The vision has resonated deeply with people and created an entry point for a conversation on poverty and well-being relevant to virtually every family in the city.

Framing the idea or vision in a way that resonates with a community is crucial to building understanding and buy-in.

How do community conversations help us create such a vision?

- A conversation between diverse members of our community over time helps us to gain a corner on the obvious. When we truly listen to one another and enter into conversation together about the system we are trying to affect, we have the opportunity to recognize the levers for change.

- When we *Listen!* and engage with the whole system, we have a better understanding of what will motivate our community to action.

- When we engage the whole system, we have a better understanding of how the system works and can find the entry point for change.

- Early in the conversation is the time to seek to find the words and concepts that all sectors in the system will understand and be motivated by. Our language changes over time and often the right words and concepts emerge.

- Through building trust and engagement between all sectors, you will know when you have the vision that resonates with everyone.

Learn and Change to Realize the Vision

Grain for grain, sun and rain,
I'll find my way in nature's chain.
I'll tune my body and my brain
To the music of the land.

— Noel Paul Stookey, *The Garden Song*

The real hope offered by community conversations is not dramatic change. Rather, it is establishing a new set of relationships that, over time, become the norm. In any community effort, the people involved learn to work together to realize a desired vision. By collaborating, people establish a new set of relationships that over time become the norm. They learn because they are motivated by the vision. And as they learn, they change. We begin to see the transcendent impact of collaboration as we see its effects on organizations, the lives of individuals, and the community.

This is why we have community conversations and go on collaborative journeys. Through these conversations, we can learn from each other, hearing the issues from the perspectives of those affected, as well as from those with the power to affect them. This equips us to realize the vision, because we have worked together to figure it out.

How might community conversations help us cast a vision, learn, and change?

- Learning and changing occur naturally when people collaborate. In many ways, the process of multi-sector conversation can be the Trojan horse that community developers depend on. Collaboration requires people to enter into a relationship with others. As they talk, they get to know each other and build a common understanding. Often they are compelled to ask, "What can I do to realize this vision? How can I personally impact the issue?"

- Dialogue is to collaboration what water is to fish.

- The tools that elevate good conversation are effective listening and exceptional process.

- Sometimes we need to go slow to go fast. Taking the time to build a commitment to the vision, and to one another, will pay off down the road.

- By reframing our approach to help people see themselves as assets in their community, we can make a profound difference in the types of community conversations we convene. When people see themselves as part of the solution, they naturally ask, "What do we currently do to make this community a better place? How might we strengthen our ability to make a difference?" Asking these kinds of questions will lead community members into a conversation with the people they perceive to be part of the solution.

• When people seek a better future with others, they become open to positive change. When they become open with others whom they perceive to be making a significant difference in their community, they are more prepared to change themselves for the sake of the vision.

Getting Started

Never doubt that a small group of thoughtful committed citizens can change the world. Indeed, it is the only thing that ever has.
— Margaret Mead

As we have seen in this part of the book, conversing, engaging, collaborating, and casting a vision are the building blocks of community conversations that result in change. Let's conclude this part by discussing the nitty-gritty of how a community collaboration is actually constructed.

Community collaboration is filled with many surprises and less than ideal conditions. Forming collaborations in our communities requires adaptability based on the conditions being faced. Community collaboration would be easy if the conditions were always perfect and predictable.

In his paper "Can this Collaborative Be Saved?" Paul Mattessich of the Amherst H. Wilder Foundation in Saint Paul, Minnesota, outlines three points to consider when starting a collaborative effort. Each stage considers the type and length of conversation required.

1. **Collaborative history**

    You have an advantage if there is a rich history of collaboration or cooperation in your community. Making use of your community's collaboration experiences will help people put their conversation skills to use and reach a better understanding of what you are trying to do.

    If there is little or no history of collaboration in your community, you will need to spend more time talking together to learn about collaboration, shaping expectations and developing buy-in for such a process with potential partners, funders, and others whose support is crucial to your success.

2. **Reputation**

    Consider the reputation of your group and its members. It will take less time to develop trust and achieve the kind of clout required to catch the attention of stakeholders if the members of your collaboration are well-known and trusted, and have a reputation for getting things done. That said, this kind of reputation in some cases may make it more difficult to have a conversation across sectors. Keep in mind that reputation can cause a power imbalance. It can also jump-start assumptions.

3. **Political and social climate**

    Consider the political and social climate that will help you accomplish your goals. If the issues you are addressing are recognizable and understood to be important, they will be easier to support. If the political and social conditions are not ideal, use conversation to build a deeper understanding of the issues.

It is helpful to keep Mattessich's three conditions in mind when considering any collaborative effort. If you neglect or lack any or all of these conditions, you can still continue your effort, but you will have to proceed with realistic expectations.

Do not be discouraged if your community does not have a strong history of collaboration, or the political environment is not conducive to advancing an idea. Go with the flow — the most divisive communities can still be great places to live. Your skill in leading community conversations will serve you well as you bring people together. It may take you longer to achieve buy-in and to mobilize the collective energy and will of the community, but it can still happen.

How quickly you advance depends on community conditions and the strength of the organizing group. A strong history of collaboration speeds the process and allows it to take place in larger groups. If the credibility of the organizing group is weak or involves a single sector, then more strategic and smaller meetings will be needed.

Here are three skills that I find most critical in advancing a collaboration in the early stages.

The **first** skill, as Peter Senge shares in his book *The Fifth Discipline*, is the ability to see the forest *and* the trees — or, to put this in terms many of us who garden will immediately grasp: to know how to nurture the individual plants in a garden while tending the garden as a whole. We must fully understand that the health of the community as a whole is critical to the success of each social change initiative. This requires systems thinking — the ability to see and nurture patterns in a community — to understand the complexity and interrelated nature of the issues. For example, raising a healthy child requires many integrated factors. Though these factors can be nurtured one at a time (literacy, empathy, physical health, etc.), a child becomes healthy only when all of the factors are working well all at once.

In the case of community collaboration, therefore, the challenge for the leadership team is not just to implement a specific project well but also to understand the social change process: advancing a community's thinking and action to change how the community acts. We call this creating a community movement for change.

The **second** skill for strengthening collaborative action is the ability to nurture the tension between process and action.

Facilitating community collaboration at times requires patience. We have talked enough; we have planned enough; now we must wait. The idea is not ours alone; the community must respond. At other times, we do too much: Ideas sprout that we do not need to attend to; we must remain focused. We have to be able to move from collaboration to action. If the plants are not growing we must intervene. If there are no buds on the plants, there will be no harvest.

A community collaboration can be so compelling that people feel it is an end in itself. The truth is that it is a process to achieve a result. We use the community collaboration process because we consider it able to achieve real changes that affect real people and improve their quality of life.

The **third** skill is opportunistic resilience. Early wins, as we call them in community collaboration, are critical. In order to realize our big harvest — the significant social change we hope to create — we need to help our coalition to taste the early fruits of our efforts. This helps maintain their commitment and energy.

We must, therefore, seek opportunities to create early successes. In community collaboration, we will seek ways to accelerate change, choosing one or two ideas with the greatest promise, and focusing our energies on them to achieve those early wins.

One group seeking to reduce poverty felt a quick win would be a reduction of transit fares for poor people. So far they have secured the city council's commitment to reduce fees by thirty percent for people with disabilities. They are now working with city staff to extend this to all low-income residents of the city. This is a small achievement compared with this group's ambitious goal of moving two thousand families out of poverty, but it has been a dramatic motivator for them.

Early wins are important, but so is having the resilience to know that if you persevere there will be a harvest.

Once the harvest begins, you need to have the energy and the will to realize the gain. But not on your own. Take the time to celebrate. This will keep everyone motivated and help mobilize even more people.

Conclusion to Part I

A poem by Margaret Wheatley summarizes beautifully so much of
what I have been trying to say. Copy this poem in your own hand-
writing on a plain piece of paper and keep it with you. If you (as I
do almost daily) reach the point where you feel at a loss for what to
do next, or feel confused, or wonder if you are ever going to make a
difference, take it out and read it. It will be a compass to keep you
heading in the right direction.

Turning to One Another

*There is no power greater than a community discovering what it
cares about.*
Ask "What's possible?" not "What's wrong?" Keep asking.
Notice what you care about.
Assume that many others share your dreams.
Be brave enough to start a conversation that matters.
Talk to people you know.

Talk to people you don't know.
Talk to people you never talk to.
Be intrigued by the differences you hear.
Expect to be surprised.
Treasure curiosity more than certainty.
Invite in everybody who cares to work on what's possible.
Acknowledge that everyone is an expert about something.
Know that creative solutions come from new connections.
Remember, you don't fear people whose story you know.
Real listening always brings people closer together.
Trust that meaningful conversations can change your world.
Rely on human goodness. Stay together.

— Margaret Wheatley

Part II

Ten Techniques for Community Conversations

Introduction to Part II

A s we have seen, great things happen when communities hold conversations about what matters to the people able to effect change. Now it's time to get down to specifics.

You are about to read ten stories about great community conversations. By sharing these stories with you, I want to give you a sense of what's possible when holding strategic community conversations. I also want to give you ideas for exploring and adapting the techniques to your needs and the needs of your group.

I realize that every method may not resonate with you, but I hope you will find at least one that does. Explore that method, experiment with it, and make it your own. I liken this to finding a good recipe in a cookbook. Seldom do I have all of the ingredients that a recipe requires, but because I know the basics of cooking, I can adapt the recipe to suit the ingredients that I have on hand. I hope you will do the same with regard to the technique or techniques that resonate with you.

Many of the conversation methods in this guide have extensive bodies of practice and dedicated websites. I encourage you to read more and learn from others' experiences.

Many of the techniques included in this section, such as the Top 100 Partners Exercise and the Peer to Peer Conversation, have been adapted by Tamarack from methods used in other disciplines. As we continue to learn and explore dialogue and conversation techniques, we will share our learnings and resources with you. Check in regularly at Tamarack's website (www.tamarack community.ca).

Great conversations can be great fun. When we relax and take the time to recognize one another as human beings who care, we begin to build trust. Once we strengthen these bonds, the difficulty of the issue we are trying to affect becomes secondary. Engaging in dialogue helps us understand that we are all in this together, working to create better communities for everyone.

That is the real power of community conversations.

What are the chances of a good conversation unfolding on its own? The odds are often in direct correlation to the number of people having the conversation. For example, two people talking with each other have a much better chance of having a good conversation than do ten, forty, or a hundred people. This is easily demonstrated by looking at dinner parties. My wife, Marlene, noticed that having four people over for dinner, as opposed to eight, makes a big difference in the type of conversation that takes place. When we have thirty or more people over, it becomes more of an event than a conversation.

The number of people in a conversation grows as community collaboration grows. It is common for community organizations to have in excess of forty people at a community meeting. In fact, I have been part of conversations with several hundred people. For this reason, it is important to consider proven methods of holding high-quality community conversations.

Many of the techniques that follow, including Conversation Cafés, Future Search, and Open Space Conversations, have generated a loyal following. However, I am no such "technique groupie." I am not orthodox in my use of any particular technique. I often combine principles from various approaches. That said, I do have my favorites, and they are the ten that follow.

For each technique, I include a story about how I used the technique, useful tips, and resources to help you learn more. These stories are not meant to be a step-by-step approach to holding conversations. They are meant to inspire you to explore the methodology as you consider holding conversations that will work for you and your group.

1
CONVERSATION CAFÉS

One of the things we need to learn
is that very great change starts
from very small conversations, held
among people who care.

~ Margaret Wheatley

For people to collaborate on initiating significant community change, they must, first and foremost, converse. Change most often begins with simple conversations. A conversation café is an exchange of ideas, feelings, and thoughts between people. It is not difficult to arrange, nor is it onerous to carry out. As the members of a community talk and share, they can reach a better understanding of one another's values and concerns. If they take the time to really listen, they can learn from one another's perspectives. Together, they can reach unexpected and inspired conclusions, which may lead to equally inspired social change.

The conversation café offers an opportunity to share our humanity so we can understand one another better. It is a simple but wonderful tool for hosting fantastic and meaningful conversations.

My Experience

It was nearly eight p.m. A group of seventy-five leaders from across the country were meeting to learn with Tamarack about communities collaborating. This was our first day together. We had spent the afternoon taking part in exercises to help us build the learning community we all would be part of for the rest of the week.

After listening to an inspirational speech given by Sherri Torjman of the internationally respected Caledon Institute of Social Policy, the leaders entered a dimly lit room with nine tables, each surrounded by ten chairs. The tables were covered in brown paper tablecloths similar to a family restaurant, and topped with a candle, flowers, and colored markers. Folk music played in the background — Bob Dylan, if I remember correctly.

Participants randomly chose their tables and started talking. Some debriefed Sherri's motivational speech, some introduced themselves to one another, and others expressed how they were feeling, by saying, "I am so tired!"

As participants settled into their groups, four waiters entered the room, including me, dressed as if we were part of a 1960s folk festival. We handed out Conversation Café menus to participants as they chuckled at our costumes. After some good-natured banter, we took orders for beer, wine, and soft drinks..

As drinks were served, Garry Loewen — the evening's conversation host — welcomed the group, cracked a few jokes, and introduced the concept of and instructions for the Conversation Café. Participants were directed to appoint a table leader who would ensure that everyone at their table had the opportunity to speak. The leaders were to use the markers and brown paper table covers to record their group's thoughts. Groups were instructed to talk for thirty minutes about the first question on their menu: "What are my personal motivations and fears about being involved in collaborative work?"

Within seconds the room was filled with conversations, to the point of overpowering the music. The participants shared their stories, highlighting their fears and motivations to the extent that they felt comfortable.

The half hour passed quickly. After considerable effort, Garry focused everyone's attention on the next set of instructions, which required participants, with the exception of the table leaders, to leave their original table and continue the conversation with a new group.

Table leaders were instructed to share the conversation that had just unfolded at their table by using the notes they had scribbled on the brown paper tablecloths.

It was difficult to stop the conversations. Garry now faced the task of getting the groups to repeat the exercise with the second question: "What are my wicked questions about this work?" (Read on for a definition of these questions.)

Nearly two hours had passed in the Conversation Café and, despite mental exhaustion from the day's learning, participants could not stop talking. Even after the Café officially closed, participants remained in the room to continue their conversations.

I am amazed at how this simple technique can bring people together. It's as if people are just waiting for an opportunity to share their stories, their hopes, and fears with one another.

Simple conversations between people who care — it doesn't get any better than that!

Tips for a Great Conversation
- Focus on what matters.
- Acknowledge one another as equals.
- Speak with your heart and mind.
- Beware of judgments.
- Listen in order to understand: Suspend certainty and let go of assumptions.
- Slow down to allow time for thinking and reflection .
- Listen for patterns, insights, and deeper questions.
- Share collective discoveries.

Six Ideas for a Conversation Café
I use conversation cafés more than any other technique. They are simple and fun, yet extremely effective. Here are a few tips from my experience:

1. **Give the room a fun feel.**
   Take time to decorate the room like a café, complete with appropriate music, mood lighting, and some refreshments. Every detail counts and can go a long way toward setting the right mood. I love it when people enter the room together and are amazed by its ambiance. There is a sense of "Wow!" The brown-paper tablecloths and markers can be replaced by sticky notes and pens, but the brown paper creates a more inviting restaurant feeling. I have created conversation cafés with themes that mimic an outdoor Italian café or formal restaurant. I have even used actual restaurants to host conversations. Your only limitations are creativity and time.

2. Choose the questions and create a menu.

Consider asking two questions. I like to begin by asking participants one that is slightly personal, such as their fears, reasons for being here, or why they are personally committed to this work. The second question is often about the work and the change we are seeking to address, such as, "Why does poverty exist?" and "How might we reduce poverty in this community?" or, "Why do arts organizations matter to our community and what can we do to promote them?" Contact us at tamarack@tamarackcommunity.ca for a downloadable conversation café menu template to use at your own event.

3. Consider wicked questions.

Wicked questions are questions that do not have an obvious answer. They are used to expose the assumptions that shape our actions and choices. What's more, they articulate the embedded and often contradictory assumptions we hold about an issue, context, or organization. Not to be confused with trick questions, wicked questions do not have obvious answers. Their value lies in their capacity to generate inquiry and new options, as well as to bring to the surface fundamental issues that need to be addressed. Examples include:

- How can we commit ourselves to be accountable for achieving specific measurable results, while at the same time staying open to the possibility that we may be measuring the wrong outcomes?
- Do we know how to build a movement large enough to

achieve critical mass, power, and diversity while also staying true to certain contentious values and principles?

3. Follow a process.

Experience has taught me that a conversation café takes at least two hours to host, and even longer if you want to debrief at the end. Here's a simple formula for a two-hour conversation:

* Welcome — five minutes
* Question One: Round A — twenty-five minutes
* Question One: Round B — twenty-five minutes
* Introduce Question Two — five minutes
* Question Two: Round A — twenty minutes
* Question Two: Round B — twenty minutes
* Closing: Group debrief — twenty minutes

5. Enjoy!

Conversation cafés should not be overly formal or business-like. I have found that the spirit of conversation is broken if you try to control every aspect of the environment. Don't worry too much if people stray from the topic — they will find their way back soon enough.

6. Debrief the event to gather information.

I have found, when I want to capture the ideas that people talk about in order to write a report, that debriefing with the group helps me gather information. At the end of a conversation café, I ask participants to return to their first conversation table. I ask each group to spend fifteen minutes debriefing what they have heard by identifying three to five ideas to share with the larger group. They report each idea to me on sticky notes that I sort out on a flip chart in columns, grouping similar ideas into themes. I share some of the themes with the larger group. After the event, I wander around the tables to see what other ideas were recorded. Often I find a gem or two to add to the themes. This list of ideas can form the basis of a substantial report. Another way to debrief a conversation is to ask the whole group, "How was that?" It is amazing the kinds of thoughts people will share.

Conversation cafés are fun! They build trust between people, and they are a great forum for hosting ideas where people desire to see what they have in common and what it is they should be doing together. This technique has a remarkable way of building a sense of "in common." It's a fantastic tool to use early in a collaborative process.

Learn More
The following resources are very helpful should you wish to host a conversation café.

- Aids for Complexity: About Wicked Questions — www.plexus institute.com/edgeware/archive/think/main_aides5.html

- Brown, Juanita, David Isaacs, et al. *The World Café: Shaping Our Futures Through Conversations That Matter*. San Francisco: Berrett-Koehler, 2005.

- The World Café — www.worldcafe.com
  - Café to Go Manual — www.theworldcafe.com/pdfs/cafe-togo.pdf

- Core Principles for Conversation Cafés
  - www.conversationcafe.org/hostCorePrinciples.htm

- Mini-Manual for Conversation Café Hosts
  - http://ncdd.org/rc/wp-content/uploads/2010/06/Conv-CafeHostManual.pdf

Further resources are included at the end of this book.

2

PEER TO PEER CONVERSATIONS

I get by with a little help
from my friends.
I'm gonna try with a little help
from my friends.

~ The Beatles

Working in community organizations can be time-consuming and difficult. People often encounter challenges they struggle to overcome on their own and may need input from others. Peer to Peer Conversations (PTP) are designed to help obtain input from a peer group in a relatively quick and structured way. Tamarack has adapted PTP from peer coaching techniques that are used by executives in large corporations. This process is also used by smaller groups of people seeking strategic input from one another.

My Experience

For nearly four years, a small group of organizations have been meeting by invitation of the J.W. McConnell Family Foundation to learn with and support each other, and talk about applied dissemination and social innovation. (The term "applied dissemination" refers to the process of both disseminating information about an existing program, process, concept, or knowledge and skills, and applying that information in a different context.)

Each organization in this group receives a substantial grant from the Foundation to help them seek major systems change and find ways to grow successful local community initiatives into successful national programs.

As a member of this group, I jumped at the chance when asked if I wanted to raise an issue for input from my peers. After all, some of the best minds at the leading edge of innovative social change were at my disposal.

Katharine Pearson of the J.W. McConnell Family Foundation facilitated this PTP conversation. She began by welcoming participants and then introduced my colleague, Sherri Torjman of the Caledon Institute of Social Policy, and me. The two of us were presenting together.

I opened the PTP conversation by thanking everyone for taking the time to help us with the issue we were seeking their input on. Then I shared the following questions:

- How can Vibrant Communities improve learning for its members?

- What is the true value of learning to the learning community that Vibrant Communities has formed?

For nearly twenty minutes, Sherri and I talked about Vibrant Communities, the role learning plays in our collaboration, and the challenges we face every day. We could have shared our experiences with the group for hours, but Katharine reminded us that our time was up. Once again, we stated the questions we wanted our peers to discuss and then opened the floor for them to have a conversation.

The group began by asking *clarifying questions*. Often we do not fully understand the ideas or questions presented to us and move our focus far too quickly to assumptions and solutions. Asking clarifying questions allows time for peers to deepen their understanding. Some of the questions participants asked were: What year did Vibrant Communities start? Can you provide examples of the kind of learning that is done in Vibrant Communities, including specific topics covered? What is your budget for learning?

After ten minutes, the facilitator moved the group to asking *probing questions* — questions that test the assumptions the group members may have. Many assumptions were framed as insightful observations. Here are some examples:

- Vibrant Communities has a lot of experience building collaborative communities — they are leaders in using learning to advance social change. Are you seeking validation from us or is something going wrong that Vibrant Communities needs our help with?

- How are Vibrant Communities' partners responding to the fact that they are part of an experiment? What is your relationship with its members?

It's amazing how many questions you can answer in twenty minutes. Sherri and I felt heard and the group was itching to move into a conversation about our work.

Before the group discussion began, Sherri and I were instructed to turn our chairs away from the group so we would not be able to make eye contact with our peers. This kept our body language from affecting the conversation. This technique is not always used in peer to peer conversations, but it can be highly effective. We wanted the conversation to be among our peers and not directed to us. Participants were reminded of our questions and instructed to speak as if Sherri and I were not in the room.

For the next twenty minutes, we listened to insights that were challenging and full of wisdom. A highly paid consultant could not have offered me the ideas I was gleaning from my peers in such a short time. I too notes furiously.

After the conversation, Sherri and I were instructed to face our peers. We were each given five minutes to share our response to their discussion.

PTP conversations are a profound and easy-to-use technique that can be facilitated over the phone or face-to-face. And they work every time!

Steps for Holding a Peer to Peer Conversation

1. **Unpack (twenty minutes).**

   The person seeking input takes twenty minutes to share the issue or challenge they are experiencing. He or she finishes this presentation by asking a concrete question for feedback from their peers.

2. **Question (twenty minutes).**

   Peers are given ten minutes to ask precise *clarifying questions* to gain a better understanding and more details about the issue or challenge from the person seeking input. Another ten minutes is allotted for them to ask deeper *probing questions* that usually start with "Why?" or "How?"

3. Group discussion (thirty minutes).
The peer group is given the chance to talk to one another about the question posed. The person seeking input is not to interrupt this conversation at any time. Instead, they are to simply listen to the conversation.

4. Reflection (five to ten minutes).
The person seeking input reflects on the process and what he or she may or may not have learned, and shares ideas about how to proceed with the question based on the group's input.

Tips for Conducting Peer to Peer Conversations
The key to the PTP process lies in getting a good question and having the group adhere to the clarifying and probing questions that lead to an effective conversation. It's a straightforward technique. Try it, modify it, and make it work for you.

- Develop a question that reflects a struggle you are having with an issue in your collaboration and on which you would really like some feedback from your colleagues.

- Avoid closed-ended questions that can be answered with "yes" or "no." Open-ended questions help generate discussion.

Sample questions:

1. *Question*: How can we get influential people on board late in the process?
   Context: We have a good group of people who have worked hard at developing our community plan. Our group is now at the implementation stage of our plan. Many of us realize that we don't have the buy-in of the influential people we need to move the plan forward. We realize our mistake in not including them earlier in the planning process, but we were not aware of this at the time.

2. *Question*: How can we encourage funders to invest in us? Context: Our collaboration is new and several funders are reluctant to fund our work because we do not have a track record.

3. *Question*: What are some ways we can ensure that the sponsoring organization can maintain its role as our fiscal agent and not feel threatened by the work of the collaboration?
   Context: Our collaboration's fiscal agent (a large service agency) wants to be very hands-off when supporting the work of the collaboration members. But they are very nervous that the collaboration may raise issues regarding service delivery in the community that may negatively impact its ability to secure resources or maintain sensitive relationships with others in the community.

4. *Question*: How can we encourage wayward members of our collaboration to be better team players or become clearer on what they will support publicly?

Context: Our collaboration works well together and we have created many excellent initiatives to pursue. Several members of the collaboration, however, publicly criticize or avoid following through on the decisions our group makes. They are leaders in senior organizations in the community who are very important to our work.

- When presenting to your peers, use the first nineteen minutes to provide a solid context for your question by describing how your collaboration got started, how long it has been operating, its purpose and key players, and the particular events that led you to wrestle with the question. Use the last minute to pose your question.

- Be honest with your group if you are unable to answer some of their clarifying and probing questions.

- Write down key ideas during the group's discussion. This will make it easier to share your feedback on their ideas in the last part of the session.

- When sharing your thoughts, focus on group discussion points that (a) made you think about the issue differently, (b) confirmed some instincts you already had about how to proceed, and (c) provided new ideas about how to answer your own question.

We have found that Peer to Peer Conversations are often the best way to increase our knowledge about the work we are doing. For most of us, the information we receive is practical and challenging. A peer of mine once asked, "Why ask an expert when you can ask someone who is actually doing the work?" Peer to Peer Conversations can facilitate the transfer of such wisdom.

Learn More

We haven't found many external resources for Peer to Peer Conversations. Below you will find several helpful places where these conversations have taken place. There are no guides or manuals. Check our website for further resources, which we will list as we find or create them.

- Ashoka: Innovators for the Public — www.ashoka.org/
- Social Innovation Conversations: Ashoka Social Entrepreneurship Series — www.siconversations.org/series/ashoka. html
- Vibrant Communities — www.vibrantcommunities.ca

Further resources are included at the end of this book.

3

THE TOP 100 PARTNERS EXERCISE

"Who invited that schmuck?"
(A moment of weakness I felt
after a session.)

~ Paul Born

Consider the top 100 people and organizations in your community that could help you realize the change you want to see. Imagine what it would be like if they worked together to change the community. This would be a dream come true for many communities.

The easiest and least effective way for partnerships to emerge is to just let them happen. I am a huge believer in emergence. However, given that partnerships take so much time to develop, it is very important to know who you want your partners to be and to develop a strategy for building these relationships.

My Experience

I spent two days developing an engagement process with a small group that would help their neighborhood work better together. It had deteriorated over the past two decades and was known to have large concentrations of low-income housing.

We started by talking about the challenges their community faced. Crime, exclusion, lack of hope, and poverty were at the top of their list.

After spending half of the day focusing on challenges, I helped move the conversation to assets and asked, "What does your neighborhood have going for it?"

We talked about green spaces and a trail network, a community facility, and an after-school program. We also talked about the resilience of the local residents, a few caring business people, and a local politician who was so fond of the neighborhood that he and his wife came to just about every event hosted there. We talked about several small restaurant owners who were vocal and active, a school principal with boundless energy and creativity, and a group of young people who were active through the YMCA.

Many stories were shared about acts of kindness and community pride. The challenges seemed less daunting once we began to recognize and understand the people and places who made up this neighborhood.

The conversation then turned to the process by which we might bring these people together for a series of conversations. We hoped to come to an agreement on what we could do together to restore the neighborhood.

The group's informal leader asked, "So who should we invite to such a meeting?"

All eyes turned to me. My immediate thought was to say that we should invite the people we had just talked about — the people we had identified as community assets. But I knew from experience that by inviting these "usual suspects" — the people already engaged —

we would miss out on an important opportunity to engage the whole community and to identify those who were really needed to transform the neighborhood.

For the next several hours, I led this small group through an exercise that I have used with dozens of groups. We brainstormed nearly 100 names of people we could engage and then developed a top twenty list for the meeting we planned to hold. We decided that the other eighty names would be entered into a database and we would track their involvement over the next year. The group believed that without this disciplined method of identifying key stakeholders, we would have embarked on a process of luck rather than one of strategy.

Steps to Hold the 100 Partners Exercise
Here is a five-step process that individuals or groups can use to be much more deliberate in building strategic partnerships. This process can help you determine the key people to engage in the system you desire to change.

1. **Brainstorm your partner list.**
   Consider the issue you hope to address in your community. On a large piece of paper, write the name of the collaborative you are involved in. Now create four quadrants on the page by dividing the page in half both vertically and horizontally.

   Visualize all of the people in your community who have similar interests, including existing partners. Brainstorm the organizations that make up the system you are hoping to affect by using the following four categories: business, voluntary, government, and people affected by the issue. List these in the four quadrants of the page. List all of the organizations (top 100) that make up the system around the issue and place the names in each quadrant. The first twenty are often the easiest, but keep going for as long as you can. If possible, identify the leaders or key members of the organization rather than just the name of the organization. Follow the instincts of the group. Do not debate every individual suggested.

Here is an example: If your issue is poverty reduction, consider the people who work for the agencies that serve the poor, such as food banks, low-income neighborhood centers, and homeless shelters. Consider the employers who hire low-income workers, both private and public. Then, consider business associations that represent these employers: for example, the local Chamber of Commerce. Also, consider all levels of government that support or fund programs that help the poor. Lastly, identify any citizen organizations that have been developed by the poor for the poor, such as a single-parent support group. Keep writing names down until you can't think of any more.

2. **Rank your list by sector.**
Sort through your list and identify the people your group knows best, ranking the list accordingly. Organize this list into groups by sector. For government, consider dividing names into national, provincial/state, and local groups. You may also want to sort by area of activity, such as health, social services, or the service industry.

3. Rank your list by people.

Rank lists by identifying the top three people or organizations in each quadrant. I find it helpful to use specific criteria for this ranking. Here's the method I use:

Individuals with whom anyone in your group has a close personal relationship receive five points. Those with lesser relationships receive a lower rating. How do you rate your relationships? If you can ask the person a reasonable favor and, because of your relationship, they would likely say yes, this is a level five relationship.

Next, I rank each person or organization for their ability to contribute to implementing the vision. Again, if they have a lot of influence or resources, this is a level five relationship.

Lastly, rank each contact for "readiness to partner." How closely does your idea line up with their thinking? Are they in the midst of a huge change with which your idea fits? If they seem to be thinking along a different path, you may need to give them a lower rating. This is not a scientific formula. Use your gut feeling in coming up with your ratings.

4. Consider whom to approach first.

Rank your prospect list by choosing the partners you want to approach first. This stage may require research. The more you know about a potential partner, the easier it is to customize the "ask" so they can easily see the need and the benefits of their participation.

In this step, I suggest looking for two things. The first is a set of names that will give you some quick partnerships, including the people you know well and are sure will join if asked. The second is a list of contacts from your list with significant influence: for example, the mayor of your city or a leading businessperson. These are people who bring credibility to the issue and who, once they are on your side, make it easier for you to engage other key community influencers.

5. Craft the "ask."

Brainstorm how you might make the approach, but proceed with caution. I have one simple rule: Never ask a partner to commit on your first visit. Use the first meeting as an opportunity to introduce your idea and try to leave only with a commitment for a second meeting. At the end of the first meeting, ask the potential partner, "Is there any other information I can send to you, or questions you'd like me to answer when we get together again?"

This five-step process is not exhaustive; it is simply a way to be deliberate about relationship building, and to identify the top organizations and individuals that can contribute to the change you want to see in your community.

As noted earlier, entering into an effective dialogue with others requires us to be deliberate in the way we act and think during the dialogue. When using dialogue to build our community, the question of "who" should be foremost in the conversation. By recreating the system that we hope to affect through the choice of who could be involved, we have a much better opportunity to gain a corner on the obvious.

Ideas for the Top 100 Partners Exercise

- The question of whether someone really is a leader often comes up in this process. How do we know this person is a person of influence? I usually ask this question, "Is this a person who if they were to invite ten of their colleagues to a meeting, seven would show up?" People of influence are the best type of leaders for collaborative process. Position or power do not define leadership for me.

- Do not be perfectionistic about this process. The exercise is a method to brainstorm and sort the names of people and organizations that make up the community system around the issue you want to influence. Do not be overly concerned about which category you place someone in. Be more concerned about capturing the name.

- The key to the Top 100 Partners Exercise is understanding the need to be strategic about those you invite into a conversation. Everyone who enters into the conversation is a constituent who has the ability to help implement the group's idea and/or vision.

Relationship Management

I find it very useful to enter all the brainstormed names into a database. As your collaboration begins to hold community conversations, be sure to capture the names of everyone who attends. Every event you hold and every conversation you have about the change you want to see is an opportunity to build relationships. Acquire e-mail addresses and business cards. These will allow you to keep individuals informed and get them excited about the work you are doing. After one year, you could have a database full of contacts, complete with information about how they are important and how they are interested in your work, as well as how they have been involved to date.

Gathering and tracking names is important to forming large-scale collaborations. In fact, this may be the most important discipline for a collaborative organization to employ. Keeping a relational database creates a system that keeps relationships current and deliberate.

What Is a Relational Database?

A relational database is like any other list of names and contact information we put into our software programs these days, except that it has categories for sorting names and organizations based on interest, how they can help, level of importance, etc.

Tips for Building a Relational Database

- Every event held in your community is an important opportunity to build your database. Be sure to find a way to get the names and e-mail addresses of participants. Consider passing around a sign-up sheet, or find a reason to send some compelling information after the meeting and ask for e-mail addresses before participants leave. If your organization has a newsletter, encourage participants to subscribe.

- Remember, this is a discipline. Building your relational database must be something you do every day and for every event. Even if you already have the contact information, you can acquire more information about a person. Consider setting a goal for your organization's relational database: for example, acquiring one thousand names in a year, one event at a time.

- Consider using the database as a way to track engagement. I can't think of a better way than a relational database to record how many people have been involved in the initiative to date, and their level of interest and contribution. Make sure this is part of your evaluation criteria.

- Consider buying a database that is built specifically for this purpose. The one we use at Tamarack is called ACT!

- Use the database! The best way to see the power of the database is to develop a short e-newsletter that provides an engaging update of your work on a regular basis. The Internet can play a major role in allowing your collaborative work to grow.

Relationships are at the core of every collaboration. They require nurturing and time to build. Being deliberate about the people you invite to a conversation is very important. Similar to hosting a great dinner party, gathering the right people can make the event very special. Having a strategic conversation about your top 100 partners can be the most effective time your group has ever spent.

Learn More
There are no manuals for this exercise on the web but we have provided two links to relationship-management software. We use ACT! but you can download eBase for free.

- ACT! Contact and Customer Relationship Management Software — www.act.com
- eBase Relationship Management for Non-profits — www.ebase.org

Further resources are included at the end of this book.

4

FUTURE SEARCH
MEETINGS

When you dream alone it remains
just a dream, when you dream
together it is the beginning of
a new reality.

~ Brazilian proverb

Future Search is a planning meeting that helps people to quickly transform their capability for action into action. The meeting is task focused.

This technique brings people from all walks of life into the same conversation: those with resources, expertise, formal authority, and need. It invites people to tell stories about their past, present, and desired future. In doing so, they discover their common meaning through dialogue, which allows them to make concrete action plans.

My Experience

One of the continuing highlights of my career as a facilitator is volunteering to help a group of people trying to make their community one of the most accessible places in the world. This group is led by individuals who are deaf, blind, or paraplegic, or who have cognitive challenges. Several of the leaders have multiple disabilities. The challenge for me as a facilitator is to communicate effectively with a group when its leaders cannot hear what I am saying, see what I'm writing, and so on. Difficulties and challenges notwithstanding, I always have the most fun when facilitating this type of group. I have learned so much from such people. The wisdom in their collective leadership is astounding.

The main service they provide is to facilitate barrier-free audits of buildings. A team representing a variety of disabilities is created to assess a building by walking or wheeling around it to experience the location and then share their observations in a report. This report also provides practical solutions for overcoming barriers. Their collaboration and auditing abilities are exceptional.

I was asked to help this group develop a strategic plan and a path forward to make an even bigger impact on their community. We agreed on a Future Search process. We had a wonderful time over the two days we spent together. The highlight for me was building one of the best mind maps I have ever seen. I keep it in my office as a reminder of this great experience.

The following is a memo we sent out to individuals who were invited to this Future Search process. The memo also does a great job of explaining this conversation technique.

Memorandum
Re: Future Search for the Barrier Free Advisory Committee

The Barrier Free Advisory Committee (BFAC) has done a remarkable job in building awareness and advising our municipalities and beyond concerning the importance of building communities that are accessible to all.

The approach has been simple and yet profound. No amount of academic training or third party learning could build such a team of experts and provide such a diverse team of individuals who experience barriers to accessibility in the community every day.

We are now asking ourselves: *What is the future of BFAC in our region and beyond, and how can we best engage BFAC and its stakeholders in determining this future course?*

We want to involve you in this process, and to find answers together. **We value collaboration, and invite you as a stakeholder and committed leader in our community to be a part of this future search.**

Our goal will be accomplished over two days using a process called future search and facilitated by Tamarack — An Institute for Community Engagement. During two days, we will: explore our achievements to date, determine what still needs to be accomplished, and decide who is best able to carry this work forward.

A key for this future search is to gather the "right" people in a room together, or in other words, to recreate the system we want to impact. To this end, we invite our friends and supporters, municipal staff and politicians, members of various Advisory Committees, local agencies, business people, and of course — our committee members, both past and present.

An agenda for the two days is scheduled as follows:

Our Future Search Question:
What is the future for barrier free access in our community and beyond and how can we best engage BFAC and its stakeholders in reaching this future?

DAY ONE, MORNING (10:00 to 12:45)

Introductions
Focus on the Past: Personal, Global & Local Milestones: We will create time lines of key events in the world, our own lives, and in the history of the future of barrier free access. Small mixed groups will tell stories about different time lines. Together, we will share stories and discuss the implications for the work we have come to do.

Focus on Present, External Trends: The whole group will make a "mind map" of trends immediately affecting them now and identify those trends most important for barrier free access. Stakeholder groups will describe how trends are affecting them, what they are doing about barrier free access in response to trends and what they still want to do.

DAY ONE, AFTERNOON (1:15 to 3:30)

Focus on the Present, Current State of BFAC: Stakeholder groups will discuss what they are proud of and sorry about in the way they are dealing with barrier free access in our Region. Small groups share these "prouds and sorries" with the whole room.

Ideal Future Brainstorming: The whole group will create a broad picture of how they would like barrier free access issues to be dealt with in an ideal future, without constraints or obstacles.

DAY TWO, MORNING (10:00 to 12:30)

Ideal Future Scenarios for Barrier Free Access: Themes identified from the broad ideal future developed in Day One are presented. Diverse groups create detailed scenarios of their preferred future as if it has already been accomplished (noting barriers overcome and opportunities seized), focusing on the specific role played by BFAC in addressing barrier free access issues in our community.

Identify Common Ground for Barrier-Free Access in the Future: Diverse Groups will post themes they believe are common ground for everyone. All together, the group determines their common future agenda and examples of ways to work toward it, while also acknowledging areas of unresolved differences.

DAY TWO, AFTERNOON (1:00 to 3:30)

Recommendations for Change, the Future Role of BFAC: Main common ground themes will be presented to group. Individuals will choose themes of most interest and join that "voluntary group" to develop concrete recommendations for future action.

Action Planning: What actions will the group take in their future approach to barrier free access? Groups share their recommendations. The whole group agrees on plan. Volunteers sign up to implement action plans.

Tips for Using Future Search

Future Search involves some key approaches that I have followed in all aspects of my work. They reflect the wisdom that really sets Future Search apart.

- Get the whole system in the room. Invite a significant cross-section of all parties that have a stake in the outcome. I often include those with the authority to effect the change required.

- Explore the "whole elephant" before focusing on a single component. Get everyone talking about the same world. Think globally, act locally.

- Put common ground and a focus on the future at the center of your conversation. Treat problems and conflicts as information, not action items.

- Encourage self-management and responsibility for action by participants before, during, and after the Future Search.

- Urge full attendance. Keep part-time participants to a minimum.

- Meet under healthy conditions. Convene in spacious rooms, and provide healthy snacks and meals, and adequate breaks.

- Work across three days (sleep twice). People need time to digest everything that happens. This is not always practical, but it's worth shooting for.

- Ask for voluntary public commitments to specific next steps before people leave.

More Tips from My Experience

- The question being asked is very important. Make sure that people have input into the question. Take the time to get it right. Make it clear.

- Getting the "whole system" in the room means engaging everyone. Consider all of the sectors that need to be involved and active. See the Top 100 Partners Exercise for more information about how to achieve this.

- Attend a Future Search conversation before you try to facilitate one. While this is not a hard technique to facilitate, it is important for you to understand its rhythm.

- This is a great process to use when building a community plan for your collaboration. In addition to building a plan, it also builds commitment.

Future Search is a remarkable method. This technique requires a lot of work, but it is worth the effort because of the magic present in both the process and the outcome. If the people with the power to act on the ideas generated are in the room, they can help make significant changes in your community almost effortlessly through their everyday work.

Learn More
There is so much more to Future Search beyond what has been stated above. Here are some resources that will help you learn more:

- Future Search website — www.futuresearch.net
- Weisbord, Marvin and Sandra Janoff. *Future Search: An Action Guide to Finding Common Ground in Organizations and Communities.* San Francisco: Berrett-Koehler, 2000.
- Weisbord, Marvin et al. *Discovering Common Ground: How Future Search Conferences Bring People Together to Achieve Breakthrough Innovation, Empowerment, Shared Vision, and Collaborative Action.* San Francisco: Berrett-Koehler, 1992.
- "Searching for Responses to Poverty." *Making Waves*, vol. 10, no. 3., pp. 5–8.

Further resources are included at the end of this book.

5

OPEN SPACE CONVERSATIONS

Be prepared to be surprised.
Don't carry in your own agenda
and, in doing so, miss some
amazing thing that could come
out of more creative minds
working on the same issue.

~ Lisa Heft, Open Space World

Open Space was created by Harrison Owen in the 1980s. When attending conferences, he noticed (as we all do) that people enjoyed the coffee breaks most of all. He combined this observation with ideas he learned while living in an African village to create a whole new way of holding conferences. These conferences have no keynote speakers or workshops. They are organic in design and flow.

This conference process can be adapted to hold effective conversations. I call them Open Space conversations. This method is one of the most versatile and easy to organize. Open Space is a way to get everyone in a group to have their say on their terms. They make their own agenda based on their passions and then organize the discussions themselves.

My Experience

The intermediary organization learning circle, convened by a major social policy foundation, was at a formative stage. There were so many issues to explore but no one knew where to start. I suggested we start with an Open Space conversation. As a member of this group of approximately twenty-five people, I volunteered to facilitate the conversation. I began by booking a large room where we could sit in a circle, as well as five other spaces in which small groups could hold their own conversations.

Three flip charts were placed at the front of the room.

On the first flip chart, I wrote: "What makes Open Space work is that we are all passionate about today's topic. Today, we are asking: What makes for a 'useful' intermediary organization?"

On the second flip chart, I wrote the four key principles of Open Space:

1. Whoever comes are the right people.
2. Whatever happens is the only thing that could happen.
3. Whenever it starts, it was meant to start.
4. When it's over, it's over.

I used these principles to make a point about the organic nature of the process and to explain how the whole technique works.

On the third flip chart, I wrote "The Law of Two Feet." This law states that if you are not learning or finding a way to contribute meaningfully, you should go somewhere else: joining another group, or sitting on your own and waiting for someone who might drop by and strike up a conversation.

Next, I placed markers and a stack of paper in the middle of the room. Using three clean sheets of flip chart paper, I created a mural on the wall that said, "Our Open Space Conversation."

When everyone arrived, I decided to let the group engage in that coffee break "magic" for an extra fifteen minutes. I found it interesting that two people came to me with an urgent look on their faces, asking me when we were going to get started. So we did just that. As the group sat in a circle, I allowed them to quiet down on their own — this took five more minutes. I began by saying hello, and introducing the Open Space process, the question, and the principles. I also asked if anyone in the room had ever been to an Open Space conversation before. No one had.

Then, I explained how Open Space worked. In the center of the room were sheets of paper, and anyone who had a topic that they wanted to talk about could write it on a piece of paper, announce it to the group, and then place it on the mural. We did this for about seven minutes. During that time people listed such ideas as: effective coaching — how to tell people what to do without really telling them; raising and distributing funds from the center; and national policy advocacy — ideas for impact. We had a total of twelve different ideas.

We listed six topics on one sheet, which we called Conversation One, and the remaining six topics on another sheet, to create Conversation Two. Then I instructed the group to self-organize. Everyone was to view the conversation topics for a few minutes. The people who suggested topics were to pick up their topic and take it to one of the other rooms. Others were to follow based on the topic they wanted to discuss. Each group was asked to assign a note taker once they gathered in their room. The person who had posed the question was to facilitate the conversation.

Within minutes, the big room was clear. In each of the other allocated rooms, people introduced themselves and began a conversation. The remarkable thing about Open Space is that it works every time. After an hour of these conversations, I called everyone together in the large room and asked the note takers to provide a quick summary of their conversation. After that, they handed in their notes so we could minute the meeting, and then we repeated the exercise for the next set of questions.

I share this Open Space experience not only because it is a classic example of an effective dialogue, but also because it demonstrates how a little bit of creativity and adaptive ingenuity can go a long way toward creating a great conversation.

Tips for Hosting an Open Space Conversation

- Creativity cannot be scheduled. Give people the space to get to know each other, engage, relax, and change their state of mind. I try to start all conversations gently. Sometimes you need to go slow in order to go fast. If people feel like talking to one another, they will do it on their own time.

- Trust people to self-organize. This may be the hardest thing for a facilitator who loves process. I love the eighty percent rule. If people do eighty percent of what we ask them to do (in the name of process), then one hundred percent of the time we should be very grateful.

- Passion is what motivates people to engage in talking about an issue with others. It is passion for an idea, not process, that motivates people to talk.

- People take responsibility for their ideas when they are shared on their terms. We should be smart and deliberate about creating a space that allows people to do this. We can assume that if people are given the chance to talk about what they really want to do, they will do so.

- For me, the Law of Two Feet is the biggest contribution Open Space offers to the world of facilitation. It gives people permission to walk and find another conversation if they feel they are not contributing or learning where they are. This can be extremely liberating.

An Open Space conversation may sound too easy to be true, but this is the magic of it. If people come to an Open Space conversation in the right spirit and are willing to talk to each other about what really matters, it works every time. The key to its success is to frame the conversation within the simple techniques that I shared in my experience. This can make a huge difference. Just remember to open up and have fun!

Learn More
Below are excellent resources for hosting Open Space conversations. The Harrison Owen book is definitely useful, as are these websites.

- Heft, Lisa. "Opening Space" — www.openingspace.net
- Open Space website — www.openspaceworld.org
- Open Space World — www.openspaceworld.com
- Owen, Harrison. *Open Space Technology: A User's Guide*. San Francisco: Berrett-Koehler, 1997.

Further resources are included at the end of this book.

6

APPRECIATIVE INQUIRIES

Appreciative Inquiry is intentional
inquiry, directed conversation and story-
telling that leads to a place of possibility.
I can think of many moments where
groups reached a profound spot with
appreciative inquiry and touched a
sense of freedom. Usually one person
would say something like,
"From what we heard in these stories,
we could" and there follows a collective
deep breath and then silence as people
consider the new "we could."

~ John Steinbach,
Appreciative Inquiry Commons

Conversation can be seen as a series of connected stories. Appreciative Inquiry is a wonderful approach to story-telling or "story hearing." At its core, Appreciative Inquiry searches for the best in people and organizations: It is a method that helps us seek possibilities in solving problems.

The diagram on the next page provides a useful description of the difference between Appreciative Inquiry and traditional problem solving.

My Experience

Seventy-five collaborative leaders joined together for a week in a learning community. The goal was to explore ideas together, hear inspired stories, and build on one another's knowledge and experience to advance the work of communities collaborating.

As the leaders entered the room in which they had worked together for most of the week, they were greeted by an inspiring quote from Rainer Maria Rilke's *Letters to a Young Poet*:

You must give birth to your images ...
Fear not the strangeness you feel.
The future must enter you ...
Long before it happens.

The walls of the room were blanketed with seventy-five hand-painted trees, leaves ablaze in fall colors. Tamarack staff introduced the session in the following manner:

"Together, we want to share our wildly successful stories about a collaborative activity that produced a surprise result and, in doing so, increase our understanding of what makes collaborations

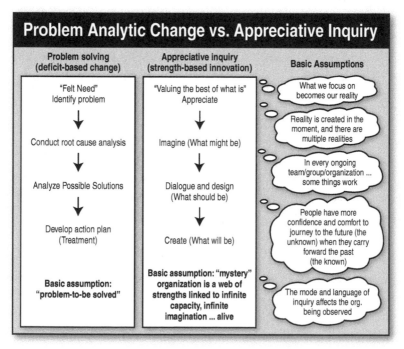

Source: Frank Barrett and David Cooperrider, Appreciative Inquiry Slides.

successful. We want to learn more about and feel comfortable with each other. Each one of us will create a visual reminder of what has inspired you to be here this week."

Participants were then asked to choose one person they did not already know and to have a conversation with them. People looked around nervously, making eye contact until their match was found.

Once everyone found a partner, we provided the following short description of Appreciative Inquiry, from David L. Cooperrider and Diana Whitney, Appreciative Inquiry Commons:

> *Appreciative Inquiry is the cooperative search for the best in people, their organizations and the world around them. It involves a systematic discovery of what gives a system life when it is most effective and capable in economic, ecological and human terms. Appreciative Inquiry involves the art and practice of asking questions that strengthen a system's capacity to heighten positive potential. It mobilizes inquiry through crafting an unconditional positive question often involving hundreds or sometimes thousands of people.*

We continued with this statement from Sue Hammond, Appreciative Inquiry Commons:

> *The traditional approach to change is to look for the problem, do a diagnosis and find a solution. The primary focus is on what is wrong or broken.*

Since we look for problems, we find them. By paying attention to problems, we emphasize and amplify them. Appreciative Inquiry suggests that we look for what works in an organization. The tangible result of the inquiry process is a series of statements that describe where the organization wants to be based on the high moments of where they have been. Because the statements are grounded in real experience and history, people know how to repeat their success.

Then we asked if anyone had participated in an Appreciative Inquiry exercise before. Several people raised their hands and shared very positive comments. Before beginning the exercise, we handed out a list of ideas for using Appreciative Inquiry in an interview. The list included the following points.

Conducting an Appreciative Interview

- The interview is intended to be a relaxed conversation. Give people time to share their story.

- Engage your curiosity about your partner's experiences, thoughts, and feelings. You will come to know them better or in a different way. Assume that you will be surprised and amazed by what you are told. You may be the first person they have ever shared this information with.

- The interview is intended to be a relaxed conversation. Give people time to share their story.

- Keep the focus on the interviewee as they tell their story. This is their turn to talk, so listen carefully. Don't tell your story or give your opinion about their experiences.

- Here are some *possible* questions to use to probe further:
  - Tell me more about that.
  - Why do you feel that way?
  - Why was that important to you?
  - How did that affect you?
  - What was your contribution?

- Here are some *possible* questions to consider asking about your partner's "wildly successful" collaboration:
  - Tell me about your wildly successful collaborative story.
  - Why do you consider the collaboration wildly successful?
  - How did you support each other's efforts? How did you communicate?
  - What are the most important contributions made by you and others?
  - What surprised you? Why do you think it turned out the way it has?
  - As you look into the future, what lessons did you learn that you will carry forward?

- And, finally, ask, "Is there anything else you would like to add?"

The group was excited to get started. They had been anticipating for some time the opportunity to share their collaborative success stories with their peers. We gave this final set of instructions:

"Posted around the room are a series of painted murals, each containing several trees. Each of you has your own tree on which to document your story. Work with your partner, and, using the principles of Appreciative Inquiry interviews, take turns interviewing each other. Throughout the interview, the interviewer will note the things that made the collaboration look successful and represent them with a word or a short phrase on a leaf of the tree. At the same time, in the roots of the tree, the interviewer will record with a word or short phrase the leadership skill, condition, or process that made the collaboration successful."

The following was used as an example:

Leaves may contain words like:	Roots may contain words like:
Inclusive	Multi-sector representation
Open	Up-to-date website
Credible	Business leader participation

As soon as we had finished instructing the group, the volume in the room started to rise. People began engaging in one another's stories, leaning in to hear what was being said. There was positive energy in the room as a result of simply framing the inquiry from seeing problems to possibilities, from skepticism to a spirit of namaste — the idea that the best in me seeks the best in you.

The group reconvened after more than an hour of intense conversation, which included people writing ideas and stories on their trees, and adding artistic impressions and diagrams. Two facilitators chose a number of compelling stories to share. They used the leaves of the tree to demonstrate what the success looked like and the roots of the tree to demonstrate the roots of that success.

Participants were then invited to "walk through the forest of success" for thirty minutes to explore each other's stories. Once again, the room filled with inquiry, chatter, and laughter.

This is the magic of an Appreciative Inquiry.

Tips for Holding an Appreciative Inquiry Session

- The words "appreciative inquiry" can be intimidating for some people. Demonstrating this technique beforehand will help quash negative notions.

- In essence, Appreciative Inquiry is the simple act of reframing the conversation from one of seeking to solve problems to one of seeking possibilities.

- Be creative and adapt to what works for your group. You do not need to go through the work and expense of creating a forest of trees. While this proved to be a wonderful and colorful experience for our collaboration, other forms of note taking can also work well.

Appreciative Inquiry has an almost universal application and is used by many disciplines. When using Appreciative Inquiry to host conversations, thinking positively helps participants open up to possibilities, hear stories of success, and focus on opportunities. This is my favorite type of conversation.

Learn More

- Appreciative Inquiry Commons — www.appreciativeinquiry. case.edu
- Barrett, Frank J. and Ronald E. Fry. *Appreciative Inquiry: A Positive Approach to Building Cooperative Capacity*. Chagrin Falls, OH: Taos Institute Publications, 2005.
- Cooperrider, David L., Diana Whitney, and Jacqueline Stavros. *Appreciative Inquiry Handbook* (w/ CD). Euclid, OH: Crown Custom Publishing, 2003.
- Cooperrider, David L. and Diana Whitney. *Appreciative Inquiry: Collaborating for Change*. San Francisco: Barrett-Koehler, 1999.

Further resources are included at the end of this book.

7

COMMON MEANING
QUESTIONNAIRES

So, just why — why are we here,
And just what — what —
what — what do we fear?
Well, ce soir, for a change, it will all
be made clear,
For this is "The Meaning of Life."
C'est le sens de la vie.
This is "The Meaning of Life."

~ The Meaning of Life Song, Monty Python

When a new group gathers to explore collaboration in their community, they often ask, "Where do we start?" My first instinct is to say, "Have a conversation!" My experience with Open Space conversations has taught me that it does not really matter where you start a conversation. What needs to be said will be communicated if you are open to it.

Nonetheless, I have created a method using a questionnaire that helps capture common meaning in a group. The questions help people express their meaning and their perception of words and concepts. The facilitator can then gather the responses to show similarities or differences in meaning within the group. I complement this exercise with asking the same participants to draw pictures that express meaning. An example of this meaning questionnaire, complete with responses and a sample of a participant's drawing, may be found at the end of this chapter.

The method is loosely based on Eidetics, a process founded by Henry Evering, an organizational and systems researcher and author of *Creating Whole Organization Synergy*. Eidetics relies on "Socratic questioning principles" that assume every individual possesses innate knowledge, a unique way of seeing things, and the ability to find solutions by cooperating with others for mutual benefit. Evering's colleague Russ Christianson has popularized this method and uses it to help groups build strategic plans and conduct market research. This Common Meaning exercise models Evering and Christianson's principles in a format that enhances group formation.

My Experience

A philanthropist proposed a challenge to a group of local arts organizations, calling on them to work more closely together to build an arts system that was healthy, visionary, and sustainable. Although the arts community already had a history of working together, they found it challenging to create a catalytic set of projects that would significantly advance the arts in their community.

A small group, which I was a part of, was asked to convene a system that develops, displays, finances, and benefits from the arts. This founding group was composed of a dozen people, including independent artists, leaders of arts coalitions, business leaders, and philanthropists. The question we wanted to explore was, "How can we build a world-class arts community together?" I was asked to facilitate the conversation.

Prior to the meeting, I spoke at length with the organizers of this conversation, and we determined that our first goal was to help the arts community agree on what they had in common. We felt this would be a good starting point for the longer process of agreeing on what they could accomplish together.

I designed the following questionnaire to facilitate the conversation.

Common Meaning Questionnaire

(**Note:** On the original version, each question is followed by space for participants' responses.)

Your Name: _____

Together, Building a Vibrant, World-Class Arts Community

1. What does together mean to me?
2. What does building mean to me?
3. What does together, building mean to me?
4. What does vibrant mean to me?
5. What does world class mean to me?
6. What does community mean to me?
7. What does arts community mean to me?
8. What does a vibrant world-class arts community mean to me?
9. Below, using all of the colors available, draw your vision of a world-class community.
10. Describe your picture.
11. Use three words to describe the feelings your picture evokes.
12. Share three ideas we could do together to realize your vision.

The group met in one of the most architecturally significant buildings in their community. After brief introductions, I handed out the questionnaire and explained that I would read through each question, allotting about thirty seconds for each question except for question 9, which was allotted ten minutes. Crayons and markers were placed on the table for participants to draw their picture for question 9.

When all the questions had been answered, I asked each participant to share their responses. We were a group of twelve, so this didn't take very long. We then posted the pictures they drew in response to question nine and gathered around them to discuss the patterns, shapes, and colors that they had in common.

A wonderful conversation ensued. We were well on our way to working together and developing a richer understanding of both the individual and collective "meaning" of the group.

After spending the morning together, I worked with our team at Tamarack and transcribed the questionnaires into the document you see below. We gathered all of the questionnaires and compiled the common words or phrases from each question. Our goal was to determine how many times the same word or phrase was used to answer the meaning question. Rachel Veira Gainer worked with Laura Zikovic to place each picture into a PowerPoint presentation and then transcribe the associated answers to questions 10, 11, and 12 to build a unique slide for each participant. See the example on page 165.

At the group's next meeting, we reviewed the PowerPoint and the report on meaning questions. It was a wonderful way for us to start the next phase of our work, which was to figure out how we would work together and what we would work on. This was an important foundation for the long journey ahead.

After sharing their meaning definitions, the group considered their opening vision statement. Then, a new vision statement emerged, after the group engaged in a short debate. This new vision statement was thought of as "good enough for now," given that, with more conversation, revised statements would continue to emerge. We did all of this in about an hour.

The following is an example of a tabulated questionnaire and picture from my Common Meaning experience.

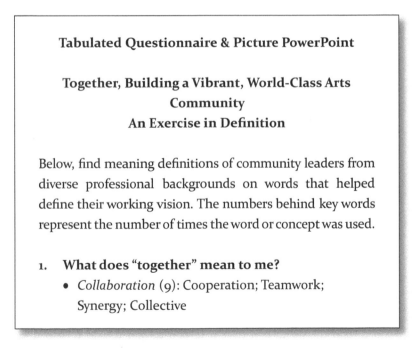

Tabulated Questionnaire & Picture PowerPoint

Together, Building a Vibrant, World-Class Arts Community
An Exercise in Definition

Below, find meaning definitions of community leaders from diverse professional backgrounds on words that helped define their working vision. The numbers behind key words represent the number of times the word or concept was used.

1.   **What does "together" mean to me?**
    • *Collaboration* (9): Cooperation; Teamwork; Synergy; Collective

- *Communication* (9): Negotiation; Open; Honest; Trusting; Sharing; Understanding; Debate
- *Common goals* (8): Consensus; Aligned; Common activities
- *Support* (5): Non-judgmental; Integrity
- *Togetherness*: Connectedness
- *Proximity*: A gathering
- *Other*: All at once; Willing; Diversity; Family; Community; Equality

2. **What does "building" mean to me?**
   - *Incremental steps* (7): Moving forwards and backwards; Progress
   - *Construction* (6): Playing with woodblocks; Physical structure; Quality workmanship; Putting "things" together to achieve form
   - *Achieve a goal* (5): Implementing consensus
   - *Collaboration* (5): Organization; Adding value; Systems
   - *Increasing & growing* (4): Flourishing; Having potential
   - *Material / resources*: Investment in innovation; Creating
   - *Solid foundation*: Critical case
   - *Other*: Edifying; Time sensitivity; Maintaining; Security

3. **What does "together, building" mean to me?**
    - *Working in conjunction to create* (9): Barn-raising; Accomplishment; Action; Engagement; Putting things together
    - *Shared vision* (8): Hope; Inspirational
    - *Collaborative* (7): Partnerships; Working in faith & trust; Developing & implementing consensus; Synergy
    - *Collective effort / teamwork* (4): Do your part
    - *Hard work*: Division of labor
    - *Communication*: Listening; Exchange of ideas
    - *Other*: Planning together, Open to change; Many possible routes; Taking advantage of opportunity; Looking outside the box; Community

4. **What does "vibrant" mean to me?**
    - *Exciting* (7): Attention-getting; Wow!
    - *Energy / Energizing* (6): Power; Moving; Stimulating
    - *Alive* (5): Vital
    - *Colorful* (4): RED hot
    - *Passionate*: Expressive
    - *Ensuring positive change*: Visionary
    - *Healthy*
    - *Innovation*: Creative; Open to risk
    - *Bright*: Shining; Sparkling; Luminous
    - *Beautiful*: Attractive

- *Harmony/Harmonious*: Inclusive; In tune; Resonant; Engaged with wider community
- *Happy*: Joyful
- *Other*: Happy; Loud; Big; Splendid; Wonderful; Busy; Challenging; Uplifting

5. **What does "world-class" mean to me?**
   - *Highly regarded* (7): Something to be proud of; Perceived standard of achievement
   - *Best of its kind* (5): Splendid; Successful; Wonderful
   - *A cliché* (4): Out of touch and "provincial"; "We want to be New York!"
   - *Model for others*: Leadership
   - *Other*: Original, Distinct/unique; Envy; Research, learning, & building; Healthy; Famously fun; Relating to the "greater mind"; Confident; Connected; Aware; Full in all respects; Nothing & everything; Foundation of society; Interactive; Educational; Inviting the world to be our peers

6. **What does "community" mean to me?**
   - *Belonging & connectedness* (5): Partnerships
   - *Diversity* (3)
   - *Open & accepting / inclusive* (3): Trust
   - *Local or regional place* (3): World; city; province; country
   - *Other*: Proximity; Living, sharing, working, loving, grieving, celebrating, side by side; Relationships

based on shared interests; Distinct; Internal; Everything; Ability to rely on others; Working together for a common goal; Organizational structure; Global sharing & global caring; Choices

7. **What does "arts community" mean to me?**
   - *Artists & arts organizations* (9): Professional & amateur; Emerging & established; Cultural industries
   - *Creativity & imagination for all* (5): Creative individuals in close proximity
   - *Audiences* (4)
   - *Patrons* (4)
   - *Diversity*: Multiplicity; Eclectic
   - *Working together*: Collaboration
   - *Vibrant*: Energy
   - *Other*: New ideas; "out there"; Different; Music, visual, dramatic, educational & historic; Educational; One piece of a puzzle; Choices; Opportunity; Challenging; Hope; Pleasure; Outgoing; Populated by Bohemians

8. **What does "a vibrant, world-class arts community" mean to me?**
   - *Vibrant* (14): Energy; Growing; "Buzz" around venues/events; Passionate; Positive; Healthy (artistic & fiscal); High-functioning; Splendid; Active; Enjoyment; Excellence

- *Global recognition* (6): Attracts peers
- *Influential* (6): Contributing to society & culture; Visible
- *Distinct* (4)
- *Leading*
- *Artists locating here*
- *Community pride*
- *Innovation & originality*: Bold; Visionary; Possibilities
- *Belonging*: Tolerance
- *Other*: Aesthetically pleasing functional spaces; Confident; Firm foundations; Prosperity; Variety; Chatter; Parts of a whole; Street life; Arts groups working together; Stability

The picture opposite is just one of twelve that were produced to answer questions 9, 10, and 11.

Tips for Using the Common Meaning Questionnaires

- Note how the questions are designed. I took a purpose statement and deconstructed it by creating a meaning question for each significant concept. For example, for the word "together," I created the meaning question, "What does 'together' mean to me?" At times I grouped words to create a meaning question such as, "What does 'vibrant arts community' mean to me?" The sequencing is modelled after the Socratic method. By deconstructing the building blocks of a

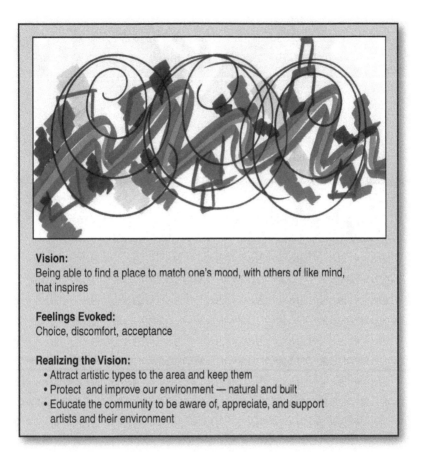

Vision:
Being able to find a place to match one's mood, with others of like mind, that inspires

Feelings Evoked:
Choice, discomfort, acceptance

Realizing the Vision:
- Attract artistic types to the area and keep them
- Protect and improve our environment — natural and built
- Educate the community to be aware of, appreciate, and support artists and their environment

statement, we can achieve richer meaning statements for the purpose statement we are designing.

- The purpose statement is the most important piece of the questionnaire, and it is also the starting point. You can work with your team to design this in advance. Or, as in my experience above, a small group can work together to design the purpose statement to be discussed.

- In the experience I described above, this exercise took just over an hour. It's amazing how much we can learn from one another in such a short period of time, and how intensely we can focus on the purpose for which we are gathered.

Common Meaning is a unique approach in which people can be deliberate about exploring words and concepts they hold in common. This technique helps participants explore and talk about the meaning behind the words. In doing so, they build common understanding. This is a great method to use when forming a new collaborative.

Learn More

There are no specific manuals for this method. Visit our website for more resources.

- Evering, Henry and Paul Evering. *Creating Whole Organization Synergy: The Eidetic Reference Book* Toronto: Eidetics, 2001. (To order the book, visit http://books.google.ca/books/aboutCreating_Whole_Organization_Synergy_the.html?id=ZuE-AQAACAAJ&redir_esc=y

Further resources are included at the end of this book.

8

FOOD, MOVIES ... AND CONVERSATIONS

"Let's eat!"

A minute passes and my son asks,
"So, how was your day?"

~ A daily occurrence in the Born–
Epp household

This is not a technique. It is a series of ideas that frame a technique for holding conversations.

The best conversations I have been involved in usually involve food — and, I admit, some wine — and friends, or even a group of people I have just met. We sit. We eat. We talk.

Movies provide different stimulation but achieve a similar effect. They open up spaces in our hearts and minds. Books and music create similar opportunities for meaningful conversations.

Tamarack has a dedicated space on its website to recognize the connecting qualities of food and movies. Our Recipes section includes stories about community and how food has been that special leaven in bringing people together. Our Movies section recognizes how movies can share positive messages and prompt us to think about the communities we want to live in. We profile movies and other forms of media that we think have a powerful community message.

Food

My Experience

A group of a community's best and brightest managers were to meet for four hours to talk about collaboration. They drove through a snowstorm to get there, delaying meetings and pressing priorities in order to participate in this conversation. The city engaged me to speak on collaboration. The city commissioner and his staff had worked tirelessly to prepare his speech to set the stage for a new way of working. Their desire was to motivate everyone in the room to consider how they could help their city become known for collaboration.

Before the event concluded, we asked one hundred leaders in the city to fill in an evaluation form about the day and to make suggestions for future events. After everyone left, the commissioner and I sat together and reviewed the evaluations. They were ecstatic about this new direction and very kind in their comments about my presentation. As we came to the last question, we realized that more than fifty percent of the responses asked, "Where were the muffins?"

This organization had spent more than $5,000 on a speaker, travel, and a facility. They used the valuable time of their leadership. When I calculated wage costs of one hundred senior managers, I estimated approximately $20,000 for a half a day of their collective time. Despite these expenses, the meeting organizers did not even think to provide $150 worth of muffins or refreshments. It was a simple oversight that made people feel less valued.

Food is to conversation what water is to fish. Consider the feeling that comfort food gives, the associations we have with food, and the fact that we tend to slow down with others when food is involved.

The way we associate food with conversation makes it an almost essential ingredient for good conversation.

The simplest advice I can give about food is not to ignore it. It is most often the smallest expense when hosting a conversation, yet it can go a long way toward lifting spirits and making people feel appreciated.

Ideas for Using Food for Dialogue
Conversations can also be built around food. Here are five ideas to consider.

1. **A progressive dinner.**
   Perhaps you want to give the twenty members of your collaboration's leadership roundtable a better understanding of issues facing your city. The issue you want to promote may be children and health. By organizing a day-long conference, you move to different parts in the city five times.

   In the morning, you start at the local school and join a breakfast program for kids who come to school hungry. You hear their story and eat what they eat. Then you move to a daycare in an upscale neighborhood where you hear what those children say over their mid-morning snack.

   For lunch, you move to Chinatown (or a different ethnic neighborhood) and meet with a group of mothers. You help prepare a meal, make decorations, and eat together while hearing stories about becoming new citizens, cultural life, and more, as well as how the children respond to these changes.

Next, you visit a healthcare center or a hospital for afternoon tea. You listen to nurses and doctors talk about the health of children. If there's time, you move to a neighborhood center and prepare a barbeque for the residents.

After each event, you huddle with your colleagues for half an hour and ask one simple question: "What does this experience mean for our work?" I guarantee a wonderful conversation.

2. A restaurant for effect.

Consider asking a restaurant to open after hours or on a day they are normally closed in order to help you host a conversation café. In just about every neighborhood there are places to eat — places where the locals feel comfortable. If you want to attract more than the usual suspects to a conversation, host a conversation café in a restaurant where the audience you want to attract feels comfortable.

I have held several of these kinds of conversations for business leaders and had a senior business leader send out the invitations on their personal letterhead (they also paid for the meal). People came for lunch and had a great time. The venue went a long way toward making them feel comfortable.

I have also marketed a conversation at a local café with a very diverse clientele. The owner handed out a flyer with every bagel sold. A wonderful, eclectic mix of residents showed up. Since they knew the owner and had been to his café many times, they entered into the conversation with ease about a rather sensitive topic.

In both of these examples, people I seldom converse with came to the venue, most likely because it was a restaurant rather than a community center.

3. Cooking together.

A favorite program of mine is called Collective Kitchens. A group of low-income women cook together weekly with volunteers from a local church using the church's kitchen. They cook seven different meals together, in batches large enough to feed all of their families. Then they fill containers and take them home to freeze or refrigerate with enough food for suppers all week long. These women support each other, learn together, form relationships, and learn essential cooking, shopping, and food preparation skills for eating on a tight budget. Their bond over food has proven to be a great way to generate conversation.

4. Promote an idea — raise funds.

Consider the need to engage people of wealth and influence in the ideas promoted by your collaboration. Seek one of the individuals you trust most and ask if he or she would host a dinner party for a dozen people. Send out invitations together. At the dinner, the host welcomes everyone and a light meal is served. After dinner, the host introduces your work and shares why he or she supports what you do. Then it's your turn to share your story and idea with the group. Everyone can join in the conversation over dessert.

5. A potluck.

I love potlucks. I think they represent the very best of community. Many simple dishes can combine to create a great feast.

Potlucks create great conversation. When you bring food for others to share, something opens in your heart. Although there is no science to prove this, my experience with many of these meals has me convinced! Visit the Tamarack website to read *Stone Soup,* a great children's story about potlucks.

Food is a wonderful reason to gather people together and a natural way to promote conversation. The staff at Tamarack have written a number of stories about community and food. We share our recipes in hopes that they will be an ingredient in your next engaging conversation.

Movies

Movies have the ability to open hearts and minds, and stimulate interesting conversations. Movie clubs are very popular today, inviting members to watch a movie together and follow up with a conversation about the plot, themes, characters, and more.

Consider using a movie as a vehicle for introducing community members to an idea. The movie can help community members understand an issue or a technique for working collaboratively in creating a vibrant community. Consider hosting "Saturday Night at the Movies" in your neighborhood or community.

By talking together about a movie, people can consider various issues. These may include:

- Understanding why a new way of looking at solving community problems is important.

- Becoming familiar with the main ideas underlying your work.

- Initiating conversations about ideas in order to engage with others who share a desire to create social change in their community. Through these conversations, people feel free to explore the possibilities of adopting a comprehensive approach for addressing local issues of concern.

Steps for Hosting a Conversation Café after a Movie
Read more about hosting a conversation café in chapter 1 of this part.

1. **Prepare.**
   Decide on the topic you want to converse about and find a movie that makes a point similar to the one you want to make.

   Here are a few examples of movies that engage important topics:

   - *Remember the Titans:* Racism
   - *Akeelah and the Bee:* Youth and community
   - *Radio:* Disability
   - *Take the Lead:* Youth violence

2. **Set a date.**
   Decide on a day and time to get together with people in your organization or community who are interested in the topic. Send out invitations.

There are many ways to orchestrate effective community conversations. If the group is small, you may want to involve everyone in a single conversation. However, if there are more than eight participants, the conversations will be more lively and productive if you break into smaller groups. To get community members to actively engage in a particular issue, you may want to invite a larger group of people from different sectors in the community. This will ensure a variety of perspectives.

3. Set up.

Organize small tables or groupings of approximately five people each. If there are more than five at the table, it may be difficult for everyone to contribute. With fewer than five, you may lack diversity of perspective.

Cover the tables with paper and place a jar of markers on each table so participants can record notes during the conversations. The paper can serve as a record of conversation highlights.

Create an informal, intimate atmosphere. This is a special event, so put effort into capturing the ambience of a café, complete with coffee, snacks, or drinks as appropriate.

Consider the questions and select those you think the group will find most engaging (or decide as a group).

As people arrive, invite them to arrange themselves at the tables. Encourage them to sit with people they do not know, in order to engage with new perspectives. If you have not already done so, ask for a volunteer from each table to be the table leader.

4. **The conversation.**
Begin by sharing information with the group that you think will be useful. You may want to share some ideas on the value of community conversations to help people understand the reasons for meeting and to encourage them to fully invest in the conversations.

Watch the movie, and don't forget the popcorn!

Once all participants have viewed the movie, pose the first question. Let everyone know that they will have two rounds of conversation on this question. Each round will last approximately twenty minutes.

Explain the community conversation format. Review the guidelines and begin the conversations, addressing one question at a time. Hold an open discussion to share conclusions from the conversations and ideas about possible next steps.

At the end of the first round, everyone (except the table leader) moves to a new table, carrying the ideas and themes from the first round into their new conversations.

Table leaders welcome new guests and briefly share the main ideas and questions that arose in the first round. The conversation continues for another twenty minutes.

For the next round, introduce a new question and repeat the process used for the first question: two rounds of conversation.

In the fifth and final round, have people return to the original tables to synthesize what they have learned. By now the room will be thoroughly cross-pollinated with ideas from all of the conversations.

Once the fifth round is complete, hold an open discussion where table leaders share the conclusions from their conversations, and the entire group considers what they have learned and what actions they might want to take in their communities as a result.

Tips for Hosting a Movie Conversation Café

- Encourage people at your table to make note of key ideas, questions, and discoveries on the table paper. Some may prefer to sketch pictures or draw diagrams. All contributions are welcome and helpful.

- Remind people of the conversation guidelines. Encourage participation from everyone.

- Summarize key ideas from previous rounds so participants can make connections and build on concepts and insights.

- See the chapter on conversation cafés above for more tips and ideas about hosting a conversation café after watching a movie.

Food, movies, and great conversation — it doesn't get any better than that. Too often we think of conversation as something we do in order to get somewhere. We separate work from pleasure, and in doing so we make the conversation too serious. Using food and movies as catalysts for conversation helps us remember that most great conversations just happen. All we need to do is provide an enabling context.

Learn More
We have reviews of movies and some food stories on the Tamarack website that we hope will inspire your community conversations.

- Tamarack: Recipes — www.tamarackcommunity.ca/g4s22. html
- Tamarack: Movies — www.tamarackcommunity.ca/g4s23. html

Further resources are included at the end of this book.

9

GIVING VOICE
TO PHOTOS

A picture really is worth a
thousand words especially if you
are asked to explain it.

~ Paul Born

From the villages of rural China to the homeless shelters of Ann Arbor, Michigan, people have used photography to amplify their visions and experiences.

I love to hold conversations that use visual aids. My good friend and professional photographer Carl Hiebert travels the world, teaching people how to document their community stories with photographs. His work reminds me of a website I recently found on a technique called PhotoVoice.

The PhotoVoice website is full of inspirational ideas for using photos to tell community stories. Developed by Caroline C. Wang and Mary Ann Burris, PhotoVoice blends a grassroots approach to photography with social action by providing cameras to people who have little access to individuals affecting their lives, such as health specialists, policymakers, and professionals.

PhotoVoice has three goals:
1. To enable people to record and reflect their community's strengths and problems.

2. To promote dialogue about important issues through group discussion and photographs.

3. To engage policymakers on the premise that, "What experts think is important may not match what people at the grassroots think is important."

My Experience

I was asked to spend six months in conversation and training with a group of outstanding community developers. Their task was to democratize one of the country's largest housing authorities and turn thousands of housing units into thousands of homes. We talked about leadership, community building, collaboration, tenant and citizen engagement, belonging, racism, and just about everything that would interest a lifelong community developer like me.

In order to facilitate this conversation, I e-mailed a memo to the community developers. (See next page.)

I received very few responses to my e-mail and began to wonder if anyone would actually bring any pictures. When our meeting began, I was pleasantly surprised: Everyone had brought at least five pictures — some even brought twenty! They could hardly wait to share their images with one another. They were already showing them before we started. The room was filled with laughter and positive responses like, "Great shot!" and "Wow! That's beautiful."

The session opened when I asked the group about their photographic experience. The response was overwhelmingly positive. They expressed their persistent hunt to find the "right" photo, and

To the world's best community developers:

Prepare for our time together next month by taking pictures of leadership that you encounter all around you every day. Fill the camera provided to you or, if you prefer, use your own digital camera. Once you have taken at least twenty pictures, take the film to be processed.

Take pictures that answer this question: What does leadership mean to me?

I challenge you to think about leadership as people in action and as a process by which people engage. You need not take pictures only of people. Other images can remind us of leadership, such as water, flowers, or sculptures. Be creative and have fun!

Bring a minimum of five pictures to our next meeting.

Sincerely,
Paul Born

many confessed to carrying their camera with them everywhere, just in case the perfect picture presented itself. Isn't it interesting how a camera can open our eyes?

The group's next task was to divide into smaller groups. They were instructed to use a large sheet of poster board and markers, to share their favorite pictures with one another and explain how each picture answered the question, "What does leadership mean to me?" After sharing their stories, they grouped their pictures on the poster board according to their meaning to create a collage.

The energy that emerged from this exercise was explosive. People were anxious to explain their photos to other group members. Wonderful connections were made when group members responded by saying, "That is so interesting because I came with a similar picture!" By the end of the exercise, each poster board displayed a rich collage of managers, positional leaders, work teams and people leading together; objects in motion; and abstract images of energy and vision.

Next, I asked everyone to describe the groupings on their poster board in two or three words and to appoint an ambassador to be the keeper of the ideas expressed in the pictures. This ambassador explained the pictures and answer questions as the rest of the participants wandered around the room to examine the collages made by the other groups.

After thirty minutes of intimate discussion and examination of these images of leadership, we got back together to talk further about community leadership.

It was unanimous. We all agreed that the photographic exercise provided a fantastic opportunity to explore the issues we were discussing.

Tips for Using Photos to Hold Conversation

- Many pictures will be brought to the conversation, each with a distinct meaning to the person who captured the photo. What makes this process work is that through conversation, participants are required to give up their individual photo and its meaning to a group of photos with a similar, collective meaning. For example, four of the five participants in a small group might bring a picture of their manager as a leader. These photos are grouped together as positional leadership.

- Allow sufficient time to prepare for this exercise (at least two weeks). This gives people time to fully experience their own lens as it relates to the question.

- If less time is available, consider coordinating a treasure hunt around a theme and have the groups take pictures with their cameras. Participants will enjoy taking the pictures together just as much as they will enjoy sharing them afterwards.

Using photos to hold conversations can be powerful. Taking photos provides an opportunity to "see" the issue as it unfolds. Over a period of several weeks, participants think about the issue they plan to talk about. They need to explain to people why they took the pictures, and in doing so, they formulate new ways of describing their issue. The tangible act of sharing photos evokes a different kind of conversation, giving it a show-and-tell feeling that makes for a rich and profound experience.

Learn More

All of the following websites are excellent sources for further learning:

- PhotoVoice websites (three uniquely different sites)
  - www.photovoice.com
  - www.photovoice.org
  - www.photovoice.ca

Further resources are included at the end of this book.

10

BUILDING LEARNING
COMMUNITIES

Communities of practice are groups
of people who share a concern or a
passion for something they do and
learn how to do it better as they
interact regularly.

~ Etienne Wenger

How might a dialogue be sustained over time? What would the value be of such a conversation?

When people collaborate, they naturally create a learning community (often referred to as a community of practice) as they work, learn, and plan together in pursuit of their goal of making their community a better place over time. The value of learning communities is being recognized by all sectors and for good reason. Etienne Wenger is a leading expert on this phenomenon. He states:

> *Theoretically, a community of practice is a history of social learning that has created a bond among people. People have learned together to do something and that has, in turn, become a social structure.*

The basic structure of a community of practice includes three components:

1. **Domain** — This creates a sense of common identity. It becomes a statement of what knowledge the community will steward.

2. **Community** — This includes the people who care about and interact with issues related to the domain. The community creates the social fabric of learning.

3. **Practice** — This is the specific knowledge that the community develops, shares, and maintains.

My Experience

I was part of the team at Tamarack that convened seventy-five leaders to advance the work of communities collaborating. These leaders agreed to spend five days together of learning face-to-face, and then ten months of learning online as a learning community. They expressed a deep belief in the capacity of collaborative efforts to mobilize communities. Their hope was that, together, they might build a body of practice to advance and strengthen their individual and organizational skills and make the work of collaborating easier and more effective for communities. By joining the Communities Collaborating Learning Community, these leaders indicated their commitment to share their own learning journey and open themselves to the journey of others.

As the week unfolded, we could all feel the energy of the group's ebb and flow. We were a big group located in a small retreat center situated on several hundred acres of organic farmland. The accommodations were sparse but adequate; the food was rich and plentiful; the people were gracious and helpful.

We began the week of collaboration with exercises like Appreciative Inquiry Success Stories and a conversation café to open up conversation and to build the foundation for learning together. We called this day "Forming the Learning Community." Over the next several days, we engaged in various forms of conversation. At times facilitators lectured, but most often we spoke in small groups. We began and ended in plenary sessions each day in order to form our expectations for the day and then summarize what we were learning.

Each evening we celebrated together in a fun exercise, such as learning how orchestras collaborate, listening to a fabulous jazz band, and learning about leadership as improvisation. On our final evening, we ate a wonderful meal together and danced late into the evening. The week's closing event was magical, complete with aboriginal greetings and cultural songs, followed by signs of group and individual appreciation. We were now ready for the ten-month period of online learning.

As inaugural members in this Learning Community, these leaders experienced:

- **Community:** A sense of the "common" emerged as members of the learning community spent time together sharing stories, experiences, and insights about community collaboration, and exploring the associated dilemmas and paradoxes of their work. This experience provided the participants with feelings of hope, support, and renewal.

- **Generative learning:** Members of the learning community moved from a place of association to a place of trust. They developed a trusting space and a state of common inquiry in which there was a genuine questioning and challenging of ideas and experiences, leading to generative learning and the creation of new knowledge. This experience provided an opportunity for Learning Community members to gain new insights and be part of shaping original knowledge to advance the work of communities collaborating.

- **Turning answers into questions:** Facilitators shared knowledge gained from research and experience. This knowledge was used to stimulate and focus conversation. The group worked together with the understanding that every learner is a teacher and every teacher is a learner. The Institute's modules deliberately used generative learning processes to capture the group's collective learning. Each session became a place of inquiry to explore new ideas and embrace paradox, dilemmas, and emergence. In essence, every interaction was an opportunity to evoke generative learning and experience community.

The Learning Community's desire was to work together to build a community of practice devoted to collaboration. They defined their community of practice as

> *a place where people with diverse experiences, and who share a common passion, concerns, and similar problems about communities collaborating commit to deepening their knowledge and expertise by learning together on an ongoing basis.*

The Learning Community agreed on the following approach to learning together:

- **Affirm what we know:** Each of us is a veteran of thinking and working in new and often innovative ways. We know a great deal already — much of it mined from our experience — and we are doing many things well. We want to affirm and celebrate what we know and what we have learned through our work. We want to wake up every day acknowledging that, together, we already have much of this process and work right.

- **Build a common language:** Comprehensive community-building work lacks a simple language that describes what we are trying to do and how. How many of us have difficulty explaining our approach to family? How do we help people understand the nature of the complex problems we are seeking to address? How do we communicate the challenges and issues precisely and how do we best reorganize our traditional responses to them? We want to begin to build a common language for our work that makes these discussions normal and part of the mainstream.

- **Highlight emerging knowledge, skills, and resources:** We don't believe in "cookie cutter" solutions to complex, uniquely local challenges. We believe that we are collectively building a body of knowledge, skills, and resources that can make all of our day-to-day work more effective and efficient. We have an opportunity to review what we know so far about doing this work; collectively reflect on emerging knowledge, skills, and resources; and support a broader process of improvement over the next ten months.

- **Build a supportive community**: One of the great metaphors that reflect the power of working together is that of geese flying in formation. While it is not entirely clear whether a goose could get to its destination on its own, we know that the chances of getting there are much better if they fly as a community. Flying in formation, geese experience more power as one cuts wind resistance for the other. When one goose gets tired, it drops back and another takes its place as the leader. Our work can be lonely, but we think it can be easier and a lot more fun if we make this journey in good company.

- **Regenerate a sense of energy, mission, and purpose:** Coming together can make learning easier and provide some much-needed emotional support. It can also reinforce our collective sense of mission by refueling our individual sense of mission and purpose. We are involved in what Jane Jacobs — the late great commentator on community and urban affairs — called "a grand effort at self-correction" of our communities and society. We need to feed our higher sense of purpose to continue this self-correction, particularly given that it often seems like we are swimming upstream in the process.

For the next ten months we learned together online, hosting tele-learning communities of practice based on a variety of topics we had wanted to explore in smaller groups. Much can be said about the value of these communities of practice. The best of course is sustained learning in relationship with people who care about something as much as you do.

Tips for Building Learning Communities

- Consider whom you want to invite and how they might contribute to the overall learning.

- Learning communities are much easier to sustain face-to-face, though a significant number of learning communities are using online resources to sustain their learning experiences.

- Share knowledge by hosting different kinds of community conversations. Use this input to learn more about the issues you are facing. Talk about these issues and document what you are learning.

- Consider asking the following questions to focus your learning:
  - What do we want to learn about?
  - What is the change we hope to see through our learning?
  - What is our theory about how that change might occur?
  - How will we know that the change has occurred?
  - What do we need to learn?

- Sustaining a learning community is no easy task. If possible, resources and time should be dedicated to the community. Consider formalizing the leadership of the learning community. Dedicate some staff time to supporting the learning community.

- Capture the knowledge you are learning and communicate it.

- Celebrate! This is a key component in the formation of any community. (See "Tips for Celebration," below.)

Communication and Learning Communities

Communication is critical in building and sustaining a learning community. Not just any communication is useful; it must be purposeful and consistent, as well. We have found that communication that helps people learn is more effective than communication that keeps people up-to-date on the work that is taking place, although both forms of communication are necessary. By creating a continual learning system, we help people engage in the ideas connected to the change we want to see. As such, we build their commitment to contributing to the idea's becoming a reality.

Tips for Communication

- E-mail is an effective communication tool because it allows us to present information easily. Be deliberate and consistent. Do not overuse this tool. Consider a biweekly or monthly communication.

- See communication as building a learning system. We recommend that you develop an annual learning plan for your community. Consider an annual learning theme and how you might use events and papers to further the learning community's understanding of the issue you are promoting.

- Face-to-face learning is critical in building trust and understanding. Use this method of communicating to build this trust, giving people plenty of time to communicate with one another. Use virtual or online learning to enhance face-to-face learning events.

- Make it easy for people to learn. People are overwhelmed today with the amount of information they receive. Animate knowledge by using quick summaries of a document and then giving people the option to download the whole thing. Use pictures to make your products user-friendly. Consider how to make each document personal and fun. Telling stories about individuals is very effective, especially if you are telling the story as a way of animating the change you are hoping others will emulate.

Celebration and Learning Communities

Expressing appreciation may seem like an easy thing to do, but it is done far too seldom. Asking for help may be the biggest compliment you can give a person, especially if you are able to express your gratitude to them in an authentic way. People need to be needed, and they want to know that their help has made a difference.

Tips for Celebration

- As a leader, expressing your appreciation may be the most important thing you can do. This may sound easy, but it isn't. As we get caught up in the pressures of our job, working fifty-hour weeks, and when things are taking longer than they should, we become depleted and tired. Over time, we lose energy and a sense of gratitude. "Thank you" and "please" are often replaced with, "They did not follow through," or "They could have done better." Even worse, we replace a spirit of generosity with a spirit of blame. Guard against this. Consider hiring a professional coach or asking a mentor to coach you through this leadership process. This will help you maintain a spirit of appreciation and generosity.

- Use your communication and learning events to show appreciation. Consider profiling a leader and their work. Mention a few people during your introductory comments at a community or leadership roundtable meeting.

- Hold an annual celebration event where you recognize people and collective accomplishments.

- Establish awards and make them generous and unique. We once had a famous artist donate prints of a painting with a "working together" theme to give to important people. It was interesting how these types of awards became a vehicle to show appreciation and motivate others in the community. People love to be part of thankful organizations.

- Be personal and care about people in every aspect of their lives. Go to funerals, send flowers, buy lunch. Ask people how things are going and take the time to hear what is really happening with their children, in their extended family, or with their health. Try to remember ways to care. Caring, of course, is the most authentic thank you.

Learn More

- Wenger, Etienne. "Communities of Practice: A Brief Introduction" — www.ewenger.com/theory

- Wenger, Etienne, Richard A. McDermott, and William M. Snyder. *Cultivating Communities of Practice: A Guide to Managing Knowledge.* Boston: Harvard Business School Publishing, 2002.

- Wheatley, Margaret. "Supporting Pioneering Leaders as Communities of Practice: How to Rapidly Develop New Leaders in Great Numbers." 2002 — www.margaretwheatley. com/articles/supportingpioneerleaders.html

Further resources are included at the end of this book.

Conclusion

In the middle of an intense project we were working on, a friend of mine shared these words, in a high-pitched voice, as he scrunched up his face: "Martha, do you want it perfect or on time?" We laughed together and moved on.

I don't want you to feel stressed about getting a technique just right. We don't need to get community conversations, as described in Part I, perfect. Furthermore, the techniques, as outlined in Part II, however helpful they may be, are just techniques. Do prepare, but also trust yourself and your experience; bring your own creativity to the process and combine techniques.

Enter into each conversation as if you were going on a journey of exploration. But always remember this: What is most important is that you are all talking.

Joe Schaeffer says it like this:

> *Sometimes a decision isn't necessary.*
>
> *Sometimes a decision has little, if any, effect in relation to a fundamental concern.*
>
> *Sometimes we can turn to finer details to become familiar with each other.*
>
> *Sometimes we can choose to live among those who share similar meanings.*
>
> *Sometimes we have to stay together and live with our differences.*
>
> *Sometimes we can explore an issue without coming to a decision.*
>
> *Sometimes the simplest way is the best way.*
>
> *Sometimes we can try arbitrary decisions for a while.*

Also, when you enter into conversation with others, try not to be stressed about the outcome. Here again, the Open Space philosophy — what happens was meant to happen — has served me well. Sometimes in dialogue, it's important to say, "This is good enough for now. Let's test what's been said, see what happens, and then talk again." It's important to remember that not every great idea needs to be a complete thought. It may just be a feeling that we all have and cannot fully articulate. Going with that feeling and "testing it" is an important part of formulating the right idea.

In Belfast, Father Cavanaugh told us a story about members of the community who really wanted to build a theater in order to showcase the historical events that were causing many of the community's troubles. They believed that dramas with humor and creative imagery would be the best way to portray the events and address sensitive issues.

When Father Cavanaugh set out to build a theater, he didn't organize a large committee to discuss the idea, formulate a plan, and build on it. He decided to host several plays involving young people and see how the community responded. Eventually, a theater of a relatively simple construction was built. Father Cavanaugh started many projects this way, using the act of testing an idea as an important way to start a conversation and build support. His belief was that people often need to experience something before they can express whether or not they want it.

As he demonstrated, we don't always need answers or to come to a conclusion in order to accomplish great things. Sometimes we just need to start talking and see where things go. By embracing this notion, we can take the pressure off a group that is trying to engage in dialogue.

Let me close this book with an experience I had on the east coast, one that emphasizes the importance of the people in conversation and the fact that they are unique and special. After all, the techniques are not why we are having a conversation. The people are the reason, the idea is the topic, and the technique is the approach.

I was in a beautiful village on the edge of a beautiful national park. It may be one of the most beautiful places on earth. I had been asked to facilitate conversations and provide training on collaboration among government leaders, college representatives, and economic developers for an entire week.

Getting ready for these conversations energized us because we had the luxury of being able to plan the venue, the agenda, and the meals — every aspect of the week.

We had planned a conversation café for Wednesday night after dinner. I spent two hours preparing the room, went to buy some after-dinner liqueurs, and arranged to have beautifully prepared baked-apple and partridgeberry ice cream sundaes delivered to the room. The lights were low, the tables had tablecloths on them, there was an order and symmetry to the place.

I love conversation cafés and wanted to do this one just right. I had prepared special menus to place on each table that had the questions we planned to discuss in the place of where the food is normally listed. I had even prepared a PowerPoint presentation to explain the process, embedding a picture of a Parisian café in it. As I stood back waiting for the participants, I admired my work. Perfect! I thought. All we need is the people.

All we need is the people?

That thought stopped me and placed me into that temporal space of knowing. If there was one thing the people in this beautiful area had taught me, it was that we can get so caught up in all the trappings of success that we fail to open ourselves to one another in the spirit of hospitality and welcome. This reframed the moment for me. Instead of ensuring that we would be doing it all perfectly (which of course meant my way), I decided I would open myself to how the conversation might unfold. I would engage with the people who came.

The evening was magical. Bob (not his real name) arrived a bit early, bringing his guitar with him. He was planning a singalong after the conversation café. (We had one of these just about every night — it's a bit of a maritime thing, I'm told.) As I had made the mental shift from event to people, I engaged in a fun conversation with him about music and singing and how much I had enjoyed his leadership in initiating singing each evening. I had learned in talking to him that he was a closet classical guitarist. He pulled out his guitar and played a bit of that style of music for me just as others were entering the room. He went on to play that and other styles during the first round of the conversation, as well. He brought a magic to the event that no meeting technique could have done.

People came to the talk at various times. No one was on time, but with the music, and the people enjoying their sundaes and talking, it didn't matter. We started when we started, and we moved to the next conversation when people were ready. No, a classic conversation café was not held. But did it matter?

The evening became the highlight of the week for almost all in attendance. To be honest, it had little to do with me (another moment of knowing). It was the relationship between all of us that really mattered; we had built trust and opened ourselves to one another. The space was pleasant, the idea and questions well crafted, the technique was perfect. But in the end, the real magic was in the exploration of new seas together — in the group bonding, being present in the moment together, and forging trust.

RESOURCES FOR COMMUNITY CONVERSATIONS

We have created a section on our Tamarack website that provides engaging updates and highlights on conversation, with up-to-date links and resources. Visit our website at www.tama rackcommunity.ca or e-mail us at tamarack@tamarackcommunity. ca for more information.

Organizations and Communities
To learn more about the organizations and communities mentioned in this book, visit:

Brookfield, Belfast
- The Flax Trust — www.flaxtrust.com

Community Opportunities Development Association (CODA)
* Merged in 1996 with Lutherwood
- Lutherwood website — www.lutherwood.ca

Hamilton, ON
- Vibrant Communities Hamilton — www.tamarackcom munity.ca/g2s2g.html

- Tacking Poverty in Hamiltion — www.hamiltonpoverty.ca/

Kitchener-Waterloo Barrier Free Access Committee (K-W BFAC)
* Now called the Grand River Accessibility Advisory Committee (GRAAC)
- Grand River Accessibility Advisory Committee (GRAAC) — www.graac.ca/
- Terms of Reference for the Grand River Accessibility Advisory Committee — www.graac.ca/GRAACtermsOfReference

Opportunities 2000
* Now called Opportunities Waterloo Region
- Opportunities Waterloo Region website — www.owr.ca

Saint John, NB
- Vibrant Communities Saint John — www.tamarackcommunity.ca/g2s28.html

Surrey, BC
- Vibrant Communities Surrey — www.tamarackcommunity.ca/g2s2a.html
- Vibrant Surrey — www.vibrantsurrey.ca

Victoria, BC/Quality of Life CHALLENGE
- The Quality of Life CHALLENGE — www.communitycouncil.ca/initiatives/qolc.html
- Victoria's Quality of Life CHALLENGE — www.tamarackcommunity.ca/g2s2d.html

Authors and Thinkers
To learn more about the people mentioned in this book, see:

Aspen Institute's Roundtable on Community Change
- Roundtable on Community Change website — www.aspen institute.org/site/c.huLWJeMRKpH/b.612045/k.4BA8/ Roundtable_on_Community_Change.htm

David Bohm
- Bohm, David. *On Dialogue*. London: Routledge, 1996.
- Bohm, David. "Dialogue: A Proposal." 1991 — www.infed. org/archives/e-texts/bohm_dialogue.htm
- Bohm dialogue website — www.david-bohm.net/dialogue

Juanita Brown and David Isaacs
- Brown, Juanita, David Isaacs, et al. *The World Café: Shaping Our Futures Through Conversations That Matter*. San Francisco: Berrett-Koehler, 2005.

David L. Cooperrider
- Cooperrider, David L., Diana Whitney, and Jacqueline Stavros. *Appreciative Inquiry: The Handbook* (w/ CD). Euclid, OH: Crown Custom Publishing, 2003.
- Cooperrider, David L. and Diana Whitney. *Appreciative Inquiry: Collaborating for Change*. San Francisco: Barrett-Koehler, 1999.
- Cooperrider, David L. and Diana Whitney. "Appreciative Inquiry: A Positive Revolution in Change." In Holman,

Peggy and Tom Devane, eds. *The Change Handbook,*
Berrett-Koehler, pp. 245–63.

Sue Annis Hammond
* Hammond, Sue Annis. *The Thin Book of Appreciative Inquiry.* Plano, TX: Thin Book Publishing, 1998.
* Hammond, Sue Annis and Cathy Royal. *Lessons from the Field: Applying Appreciative Inquiry,* rev. ed. Plano, TX: Thin Book Publishing, 2001.

Lisa Heft
* Opening Space website — www.openingspace.net/papers_facilitation_OSCollaborationCommunication.shtml

Carl Hiebert
* Hiebert, Carl. *Gift of Wings: An Aerial Celebration of Canada.* Erin, ON: Boston Mills Press, 1995.
* Gift of Wings website by Carl Hiebert — www.giftofwings.ca
* Tamarack: Carl Hiebert — www.tamarackcommunity.ca/g4s14.html

William Isaacs
* Isaacs, William. *Dialogue and the Art of Thinking Together: A Pioneering Approach to Communicating in Business and in Life.* New York: Doubleday, 1999.
* Dialogos — www.dialogos.com

Paul W. Mattessich
* Mattessich, Paul W., Marta Murray-Close, and Barbara R. Monsey. *Collaboration: What Makes It Work?* St. Paul, MN: Amherst H. Wilder Foundation, 1992.

- Mattessich, Paul W. "Can this Collaborative Be Saved? Twenty Factors That Can Make or Break Any Group Effort." 2003 — www.nhi.org/online/issues/129/savecollab.html

Margaret Mead
- The Institute for Intercultural Studies website — www.interculturalstudies.org

Orpheus Orchestra
- Orpheus Chamber Orchestra website — www.orpheusnyc.org
- Seifter, Harvey. "The Conductor-less Orchestra," *Leader to Leader*, no. 21, summer 2001 — www.life-bv.nl/pdf/conductorlessorchestra.PDF

Rainer Maria Rilke
- Rilke, Rainer Maria. *Letters to a Young Poet*. M.D. Herter Norton, transl. New York: Norton, 1993. www.carrothers.com/rilke_main.htm
- The Poet Academy — www.poets.org/

Joseph Schaeffer
- Schaeffer, Joseph. *The Stone People: Living Together in a Different World*. Waterloo, ON: Forsyth Publications, 1996.
- Schaeffer, Joseph. "First Notes: Making Decisions Together" — www.tamarackcommunity.ca/downloads/schaeffer/decisions.pdf
- www.tamarackcommunity.ca/g4s13.html

Etienne Wenger
- Wenger, Etienne. "Communities of Practice: A Brief Intro-
  duction." — www.ewenger.com/theory
- Wenger, Etienne, Richard A. McDermott, and William M.
  Snyder. *Cultivating Communities of Practice: A Guide to
  Managing Knowledge.* Boston: Harvard Business School
  Publishing, 2002.

Margaret Wheatley
- Margaret Wheatley official website — www.margaret
  wheatley.com
- Wheatley, Margaret. *Finding Our Way: Leadership for an
  Uncertain Time.* San Francisco: Berrett-Koehler, 2005.
- Wheatley, Margaret. *Turning to One Another: Simple
  Conversations to Restore Hope in the Future.* San Francisco:
  Berrett-Koehler, 2002.
- Wheatley, Margaret. "Supporting Pioneering Leaders as
  Communities of Practice: How to Rapidly Develop New
  Leaders in Great Numbers." 2002 — www.margaret
  wheatley.com/articles/supportingpioneerleaders.html
- Wheatley, Margaret. "Relying on Human Goodness." *Sham-
  bala Sun*, summer 2001 — www.margaretwheatley.com/
  articles/relyingonhumangoodness.html
- Wheatley, Margaret. "Turning to One Another." Keynote
  address, Kansas Health Foundation 2000 Leadership Institute, spring 2000 — www.margaretwheatley.com/articles/
  turningtooneanother.html
- Gainer, Rachel Veira. "Changing the World," *Engage*, vol.3,
  no. 22 — www.tamarackcommunity.ca/downloads/engage/
  vol3issue22.pdf

Techniques

Visit the Tamarack website for more about each technique — www. tamarackcommunity.ca

Conversation Café

- Brown, Juanita, David Isaacs, et al. *The World Café: Shaping Our Futures Through Conversations That Matter*. San Francisco: Berrett-Koehler, 2005.
- Conversation Café website — www.conversationcafe.org
- The Complete Hosting Manual — www.conversationcafe. org/host/CompleteManual.htm
- The World Café — www.theworldcafe.com
- Café to Go manual — www.theworldcafe.com/pdfs/cafe-togo.pdf
- Sample Café menu — www.tamarackcommunity.ca/CCI/ CCI_downloads/Cafe_Menu.pdf

Peer to Peer Conversations

There are no specific guides, but inspiration can be found at:
- Ashoka: Innovators for the Public: www.ashoka.org
- Social Innovation Conversations: Ashoka Social Entrepreneurship Series — www.siconversations.org/series/ashoka. html

Identify the System You Desire to Engage
The Top 100 Partners Exercise

No guide is currently available; check our website for updates.
- ACT! Contact and Customer Relationship Management Software — www.act.com
- eBase Relationship Management for Non-profits — www. ebase.org

Future Search
- Future Search Network — www.futuresearch.net
- Weisbord, Marvin and Sandra Janoff. *Future Search: An Action Guide to Finding Common Ground in Organizations and Communities*. San Francisco: Berrett-Koehler, 2000.
- Weisbord, Marvin et al. *Discovering Common Ground: How Future Search Conferences Bring People Together to Achieve Breakthrough Innovation, Empowerment, Shared Vision, and Collaborative Action*. San Francisco: Berrett-Koehler, 1992.
- "Searching for Responses to Poverty." *Making Waves*, vol. 10, no. 3., pp. 5–8 — www.tamarackcommunity.ca/downloads/ learning_center/MW100305.pdf

Open Space
- Heft, Lisa. Open Space website — www.openingspace.net
- Owen, Harrison. *The Practice of Peace: A Program for Peace-makers*. Hyman Systems Dynamics Institute, 2004.
- Owen, Harrison. *Open Space Technology: A User's Guide*. San Francisco: Berrett-Koehler, 1997.
- Owen, Harrison. *Expanding Our Now: The Story of Open Space Technology*. San Francisco: Berrett-Koehler, 1997.
- Open Space World Technology — www.openspaceworld.org
- Open Space and the Practice of Peace website — www. openspaceworld.com
- The Co-Intelligence Institute: Open Space Technology — www.co-intelligence.org/P-Openspace.html

Sharing Our Success Stories Using Appreciative Inquiry
- Appreciative Inquiry Commons — www.appreciativeinquiry. case.edu

- Barrett, Frank J. and David L. Cooperrider. "AI Workshop Slides." Appreciative Inquiry Partners. June 29, 2006 — www.appreciativeinquiry.case.edu/practice/toolsModel-sPPTsDetail.cfm?coid=9427
- Barrett, Frank J. and Ronald E. Fry. *Appreciative Inquiry: A Positive Approach to Building Cooperative Capacity.* Chagrin Falls, OH: Taos Institute Publications, 2005.
- Cooperrider, David L., Diana Whitney, and Jacqueline Stavros. *Appreciative Inquiry Handbook* (w/ CD). Euclid, OH: Crown Custom Publishing, 2003.
- Cooperrider, David L. and Diana Whitney. *Appreciative Inquiry: Collaborating for Change.* San Francisco: Barrett-Koehler, 1999.
- Cooperrider, David and Diana Whitney. "Appreciative Inquiry: A Positive Revolution in Change." In Holman, Peggy and Tom Devane (eds.). *The Change Handbook,* San Francisco: Berrett-Koehler Publishers, pp. 245–63.
- Royal, Cathy and Sue Annis Hammond. *Lessons from the Field: Applying Appreciative Inquiry*, rev. ed. Plano, TX: Thin Book Publishing, 2001.

Common Meaning
- "Creating Whole Organization Synergy: A Book Review" — http://books.google.ca/books/aboutCreating_Whole_Organization_Synergy_the.html?id=ZuE-AQAACAAJ&redir_esc=y
- Evering, Henry and Paul Evering. *Creating Whole Organization Synergy: The Eidetic Reference Book.* Toronto: Eidetics, 2001.

Food and Movies to Facilitate Conversation
- Tamarack Recipes — www.tamarackcommunity.ca/g4s22. html
- Tamarack Movies — www.tamarackcommunity.ca/g4s23. html

Conversations That Give Voice to Photos
- PhotoVoice (three uniquely different websites)
  - www.photovoice.com
  - www.photovoice.org
  - www.photovoice.ca
- Women and a Fair Income: A Photovoice Exhibition — www.albertasocialforum.ca/session/2/12.html
- PhotoVoice at BU's Center for Psychiatric Rehabilitation — www.bu.edu/cpr/photovoice/photovoice-about.html

Building a Learning Community to Sustain the Conversation
- Wheatley, Margaret. "Supporting Pioneering Leaders as Communities of Practice: How to Rapidly Develop New Leaders in Great Numbers." 2002 — www.margaretwheatley. com/articles/supportingpioneerleaders.html
- Wenger, Etienne. "Communities of Practice: A Brief Intro-duction" — www.ewenger.com/theory
- Wenger, Etienne, Richard A. McDermott, and William M. Snyder. *Cultivating Communities of Practice: A Guide to Managing Knowledge.* Boston: Harvard Business School Publishing, 2002.aszx

About Tamarack – An Institute for Community Engagement

Tamarack is a dynamic organization that engages citizens and institutions in working collaboratively to solve major community challenges. Our work exists to help us and others learn from and share these experiences.

Tamarack's Learning Center provides resources and practical tools to help local networks build vibrant and engaged communities. We produce an online magazine, Engage!, and have become known for organizing and hosting engaging learning events, including the Communities Collaborating Institute, the Collaborative Leadership Retreat, and popular tele-learning series, featuring guest speakers such as Margaret Wheatley, David Chrislip, and Etienne Wenger.

About the Author

Paul Born

As President and Co-founder of Tamarack, Paul has worked with many organizations and communities to develop innovative and sustainable ideas that motivate people to collaborative action and change. Paul also founded and was the Executive Director of the Community Opportunities Development Association (CODA) — now called Lutherwood — one of Canada's most successful community economic-development organizations. As the Founder of Opportunities 2000, Paul led a Millennium campaign to reduce poverty in Waterloo Region to the lowest in Canada, which was recognized as one of the United Nations' "Best Practices" worldwide, in 1998.

Paul holds a master's degree in Leadership, and is often invited to contribute to learning events as a keynote speaker, trainer, and facilitator on issues including community collaboration and engagement, innovation, and social change.